Connecting Curriculum,
Linking Learning

Connecting Curriculum, Linking Learning

Deborah Fraser, Viv Aitken and Barbara Whyte

NZCER PRESS
2013

NZCER Press

New Zealand Council for Educational Research

Po Box 3237, Wellington

National Library of New Zealand Cataloguing-in-Publication Data

Fraser, Deborah.

Connecting curriculum, linking learning / Deborah Fraser, Viv Aitken and Barbara Whyte. Includes bibliographical references and index.

ISBN 978-1-927151-88-4

1. Interdisciplinary approach in education—New Zealand. 2. Arts in education—New Zealand. l. Aitken, Viv. ll. Whyte, Barbara. lll. Title.

375.000993 —dc 23

Designed by Lynn Peck, Central Media

Printed by Wakefields

Distributed by NZCER

PO Box 3237, Wellington

www.nzcer.org.nz

Cover image by Santiago Ramón y Cajal (1852–1934), drawn from a histological stain of a human retinal cell.

Tell me, what is it you plan to do
With your one wild and precious life?

(Mary Oliver, from *The Summer Day*)

Dedication

To our parents, who would have loved to learn like this; and to children today who deserve an education that challenges and enriches them.

Contents

Figures and Tables

Acknowledgements

Graham Price was part of the research team in this project. His contribution was invaluable. He features at various points in this book as an invited expert to classrooms and as a fellow researcher. Additionally, he provided guidance on photographs and visual art resources.

NZCER supported the project upon which this book is primarily based. We are grateful to them for recognising the value of the arts and integration and for enabling innovative research.

We are indebted to the teachers and children who feature in this book for allowing us into their classrooms and, in many respects, into their hearts and minds. We learned much from their insights and admired their willingness to share their fears as well as their joys.

CHAPTER ONE

A Legacy of Creativity and Innovation

Deborah Fraser

Introduction

New Zealand is a remarkable little country and our achievements are among the best in the world. This is the country that has produced internationally acclaimed writers (e.g., Margaret Mahy, Janet Frame, Joy Cowley, Lynley Dodd, Keri Hulme), artists (e.g., Cliff Whiting, Robyn Kahukiwa) and dancers (e.g., Neil Ieremia); Nobel Prize winners (e.g., Ernest Rutherford and Alan MacDiarmid for chemistry); a Fields Medal winner (Vaughan Jones); top-class singers and musicians (e.g., Tim and Neil Finn, Dame Kiri Te Kanawa, Kimbra, Tiki Tane); intrepid explorers (e.g., Sir Edmund Hillary, Sir Peter Blake); sports achievers second to none (e.g., Valerie Adams, Mahe Drysdale, the All Blacks, the Silver Ferns); film makers and entertainers who continue to impress the world (e.g., Peter Jackson, Jane Campion, Sam Neill, Rhys Darby, Bret McKenzie, Jools and Linda Topp); and a whole host of fashion designers and wine makers (too numerous to mention) who keep winning top international awards.

These people are exceptional in their respective fields. Some of these fields require strength in numeracy or literacy, but many of these people shine in other areas, from the physical to the aesthetic. For a small country we punch way above our weight. Moreover, our resourcefulness is a well-known national character trait. We are the inventors of a huge range of impressive things including the electric fence, the disposable syringe, the mountain buggy, spreadable butter, the Hamilton jet-boat, milking machines and seismic base isolators. John Britten designed the world-beating Britten superbike working out of his concrete block shed. It was the first motorbike of its kind made largely from carbon fibre and it still holds the 1000 cc motorbike land speed record.

Despite all these innovative outcomes, for some reason we look overseas for what we think might improve our achievement. But Western educational policies do not reflect the diversity of excellence revealed above. Instead, they reflect a narrowing of curriculum. This includes assessment-driven teaching, reporting to standards and a pronounced emphasis on individual learning in numeracy and literacy. This trend in educational policy has led some to claim that progressive education is dead (in the UK, see Lowe, 2007) and that curriculum integration largely eludes schools (in the US, see Beane, 2005). For some years New Zealand seemed to be immune to the narrow and soul-less restrictions evident elsewhere. As this book goes to press this is clearly not the case.

We should not assume that what is happening elsewhere is superior, such as the introduction of national standards in the UK, US and Australia, which have been rolled out without trial in this country. New Zealand already scores highly in major international studies such as TiMMs, PIRLS and PISA, so it is curious, to say the least, that more emphasis on literacy and numeracy is deemed necessary. We already had a healthy combination of standards and innovation, which meant that teachers could use their initiative and not be suffocated by a narrow and restrictive curriculum.

As a country we do have a wide spread of achievement, but not as wide as some. If we are really serious about improving learning for all students we need research-based practice on what grows students' learning. The chapters in this book are explicit examples of this. We also need to reflect on what we have already achieved. In keeping with our character of resourcefulness, here are some of the things we do well in education.

We have an internationally recognised education system that, at its best, is holistic, responsive and inclusive. For example, Professor Marie Clay's Reading Recovery programme has received countless national and international accolades. Sylvia Ashton-Warner became world renowned for her organic method of teaching, which she developed in remote rural areas of the country, mostly with Māori children. Reflections of her work are found in primary schools country-wide, and the approach called "language experience" draws much from her legacy. Noteworthy are the ways in which Māori children progressed in her classes as they read and wrote stories of meaning and significance to their lives. Also in rural New Zealand, Elwyn Richardson (1972, 2012) has contributed much to our reputation as innovators in pedagogy. His focus on art, science and writing with children resulted in his seminal work *In the Early World*, which speaks across time and place to anyone interested in quality learning. He is probably our most well-known advocate of curriculum integration, and his work with children shows how outstanding the results were.

It is tempting to think that Ashton-Warner and Richardson were well before their time in terms of innovation and are unique examples of creative pedagogy. However, that is not the case. New Zealand has a long history of progressive education, which has been encouraged by education officials since the early 20th century (Jones & Middleton, 2009). This emphasis on progressive education gave teachers considerable latitude in their approach to both pedagogy and curriculum. For example, the public school syllabus in 1937 promoted the following liberal policy:

> There still survives in the schools a great deal of the old-fashioned formalism that regarded education more as a mechanical process than as a means of securing for every child the fullest possible spiritual, mental and physical development. It is hoped that the present Syllabus will give encouragement to those teachers—and fortunately there are many of them—who regard the child not as inanimate clay in the hands of the potter, or as an empty vessel sent them for filling, but as a soul, a personality, capable of being developed and trained for the wider service of humanity. (Department of Education, 1937, p. 65)

This statement reflects a very contemporary view given that it could comfortably sit within the current curriculum (Ministry of Education, 2007) many decades later. And while the notion of "training" is less palatable and relevant in contemporary educational discourse, the belief that education should not merely transmit information but should also respond to the uniqueness of the child conveys the progressive views of the time.

As teachers and researchers we continue to innovate. There is Te Kotahitanga (in over 50 secondary schools), which helps teachers to develop culturally responsive pedagogies that raise the achievement of Māori students. Negotiating the curriculum lies at the heart of his professional development programme for teachers. There is Gay Gilbert, who, as acting principal, dared to put the arts at the centre of her large primary school, with outstanding results across the curriculum (as evaluated by the Education Review Office). There is Heather McRae, who completed her doctorate on negotiating the curriculum in secondary mathematics, whereby students and teachers pursue content and method as a shared endeavour. There are primary teachers in the Bay of Plenty and the Waikato using the drama process Mantle of the Expert to engage children across the curriculum, with impressive results in terms of literacy gains. This book celebrates such innovation and brings together examples that show what is possible with curriculum integration.

We know that students learn best when engaged, challenged and inspired. We know that many important skills in numeracy and literacy are learned in various contexts and not merely in relation to set targets. We also know that integrated and negotiated curriculum provide students with ways to achieve ownership of their learning. Children have an innate curiosity about the world around them, and learning invariably follows when their curiosity is piqued. "The evidence is quite clear: when children are curious, they learn. It turns out that curiosity in school is not merely a nicety but a necessity" (Engel, 2011, p. 628).

When children come home talking excitedly about the latest issues they are grappling with in class, this shows that something important has kindled their desire to know more. When students want to bring resources from home that contribute to the class study, do extra at home for the sheer pleasure of it, offer to lead a group of peers, start contributing in unexpected ways, make suggestions to the class on how to improve something or want to stay in when the bell goes because what they are learning is just so absorbing, then we know that students are taking learning to heart. We know that they are curious and inspired. And we know that such engagement is a strong signal of progress in learning. These breakthroughs show that teachers have tapped children's natural curiosity through their responsive, inviting pedagogy. This book celebrates such pedagogy with examples of curriculum integration that have been carefully studied and documented.

Fig 1.1 *Year 3 child's print*

Research background

The current policy emphasis on standards contrasts with the view that learning is a collaborative process that is socially mediated and negotiated, is messy and often unpredictable, and is seldom captured by individual assessment results (Nuthall, 2001, 2007). This book honours Nuthall's beliefs about learning. It highlights the socially mediated nature of a negotiated curriculum and it focuses on the connections teachers and children make when engaged in integrating curriculum. It also underscores the role the arts can have in such integration.

This book is primarily based on the Connecting Curriculum; Connecting Learning project, which was a Teaching and Learning Research Initiative (TLRI) administered through the New Zealand Council for Educational Research. The project aimed to strategically consolidate and build on a previous TLRI, published as *The Art of the Matter* (Fraser et al., 2006). The Connecting Curriculum; Connecting Learning project contributes to the theory and practice of curriculum integration. In particular, it examined the learning that occurs when the arts feature within integrated learning contexts. It focused on the ways in which children seek, use and create knowledge when learning through integration. It also examined the ways in which teachers are influenced and wider communities are engaged in integration that features the arts. Most of the international practices in this field fall into the "good idea" category rather than the research-based practice realm. Thus, the project contributes to addressing this gap in knowledge.

The arts provide an ideal platform for integration, because a work of art reflects the larger social and cultural milieu of the artist (Efland, 2002). Integration of knowledge is maximised when cognisance is taken of how the arts reflect and inform society and culture. Indeed, culture "becomes understandable when read through its arts" and this "suggests that the arts should be centrally located within the curriculum as an overlapping domain" (Efland, 2002, p. 164).

While the arts are often used in integrated units of study (see, for example, Chicago Arts Partnerships in Education, 2009; Ewing & Simons, 2004; Fraser et al., 2006; Gibson & Ewing, 2011; Jacobs, 2004), there is little in the way of research on this approach. Bolstad (2011) argues that "it is fruitful to think about how the arts can be partnered with other curriculum areas in ways that allow each to contribute their own distinctive richness and complexity to the learning process" (p. vii).

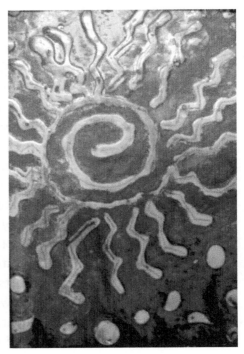

Fig 1.2 *Year 3 child's print*

New Zealand teachers have long practised various forms, levels and interpretations of integration, but the quality of such practice varies enormously, has seldom been researched and relies heavily on convenient "common sense" rituals of practice (Nuthall, 2001) rather than on a research base. This project was timely because it coincides with a school curriculum (Ministry of Education, 2007) that vests teachers with greater decision-making capacity when it comes to determining curriculum coverage, and greater flexibility in terms of subject planning. Moreover, the curriculum is founded on democratic principles such as young people being actively involved in their education, making contributions to society and taking responsibility for their learning. These goals align smoothly with curriculum integration.

We have little research that provides a basis for teachers' practice in the field of integration, and what research there is provides more confusion and dissent than clarity (as discussed by Beane, 2005; Dowden, 2006; Fraser, 2000). As Brough (2008) adds:

> Merely combining learning areas through the use of a common theme is not a stepping stone towards student-centred integration, as the pedagogical practices that underpin student-centred versions of curriculum integration are absent. (p. 13)

The role of the arts in contributing to integration is also under-researched and often misinterpreted. Bolstad (2010) found that there is considerable agreement about the need to research interactions between arts learning and other kinds of learning. Moreover, she pinpointed a need for research that scrutinises how key competencies, and the principles of *The New Zealand Curriculum* (Ministry of Education, 2007), are developed in and through the arts.

Research questions

In particular, the project scrutinised:

- the connections children and teachers make between the arts and other learning areas
- the influence such connections have on their engagement and learning
- the opportunities children have for shared decision making and ownership when negotiating curriculum.

Social constructivism forms the theoretical framework for the project: it emphasises knowledge as being constructed in contexts that are largely social in nature and reflects the collaborative learning environments encouraged in most contemporary classrooms. It also underlines the fact that children's learning is socially mediated with peers, teachers and others, within and beyond schools. Curriculum integration, negotiating the curriculum and inquiry learning provide mechanisms by which socially constructed learning is both acknowledged and enhanced.

The specific questions that frame the study are:

1. What connections are made between the arts and other curriculum areas (a) by children and (b) by teachers?
2. What influence does arts-based curriculum integration appear to have on engagement and learning (a) for children and (b) for teachers?
3. What opportunities are there for shared ownership and decision making in planning and negotiating the curriculum?
4. How do schools foster integrated projects, founded on the arts, that maximise engagement with their communities?

Methodology and analysis

Because this study focused on only a few teachers and schools, and the research questions require attention to the detailed, lived experiences of participants, qualitative approaches were appropriate. Qualitative research involves exploring a problem and gaining a detailed understanding of a central phenomenon (Creswell, 2005). Qualitative studies usually involve participants' experiences and feature a small number of individuals or sites. Such studies recognise the value of listening to participants' views and collecting data in the contexts in which people learn and work. There is also the purpose, inherent in most qualitative studies, of seeking improvement for those involved (Creswell, 2005).

To address the above questions, a range of methods was required. Such an approach enables the collection of robust and rich data that are systematically obtained and trustworthy.

The practitioner partners in the study were eight teachers from five primary schools. Two of the teachers were deputy principals. Two of the teachers had Year 3 classes and six taught Years 5/6 classes. All of the teachers were experienced practitioners with various positions of responsibility within their respective schools. All had particular interests in the arts and integration. The schools varied in composition from low to high socioeconomic communities, and from predominantly Pākehā/European to very multicultural.

Fig 1.3 *Interview between researcher and teacher*

Case studies of teachers' existing practice, gathered by the research team, were drawn from classroom observations, interviews, learning conversations with children, work samples, camera stills, relevant document analysis and school website information. These case studies were jointly shared between the university researchers and the teacher partners and formed the basis of the action research phase. The action research cycles had a particular emphasis on appreciative inquiry; that is, on developing aspects that fostered learning and engagement of children in arts-based integration.

The particular methods employed for data collection during the action research phase included:

- observations of teachers, focusing on teacher talk, teacher–child interaction patterns and teacher–child negotiations, using a systematic observation chart and running records
- observations of children's interactions with each other, with their teacher and with their activities during lessons
- collection of work samples (including literacy)
- semi-structured interviews with teachers and members of the wider school community

- learning conversations with children individually and in small groups—one involving the university staff as regular researcher, and one involving "researcher-in-role", a drama strategy for taking a low-status role of curiosity (audio recorder and camera stills)
- tracking engagement with an observational tool devised by the research team, which enabled teachers to tick and date evidence of children's engagement in learning
- interactive group activity—a diverse group of five children sorting and categorising pictures and statements from their study (audio recorder and camera stills).

Fig 1.4 *Children doing the interactive group activity*

Both inductive and deductive approaches to data analysis were used. A deductive approach was used when social constructivist theory and processes (such as negotiating the curriculum) were used as lenses through which to view and interpret the data. An inductive, grounded theory approach was used to remain open to the unexpected and the unpredictable, which is particularly important in research (Charmaz, 2005; Creswell, 2005). Initial line-by-line open coding of data enabled analysis to be built inductively "from the ground up without taking off on theoretical flights of fancy" (Charmaz, 1995, p. 37). Grounded theory analysis helps to keep researchers responsive to what emerges in the data, such as the meanings that students themselves construct from arts-based integrated learning.

Structure of the book

Chapters Two and Three set the scene for what follows in the book. Chapter Two provides an overview of the research carried out on curriculum integration. It scrutinises a range of research claims and issues relating to curriculum integration. It also outlines why this approach is relevant to teachers in terms of pedagogy, children's learning and the requirements of *The New Zealand Curriculum* (Ministry of Education, 2007). It differentiates between curriculum integration and thematic approaches, a common confusion in educational circles. It also highlights how negotiation features in this approach to curriculum and acknowledges both the challenges and benefits of this curriculum design.

A number of the classroom experiences written about in this book occurred within the drama-based inquiry approach known as Mantle of the Expert. Chapter Three gives readers some additional context and information about this approach, which was first developed by Dorothy Heathcote. First, the defining features of the system are described and the key terms explained. Then the practices and philosophies of the approach are discussed. In particular, the chapter considers how planning in Mantle of the Expert enables the teacher to combine student-led inquiry with a conscious repositioning of power relationships and an exploration of multiple perspectives through drama.

Chapters Four, Five, Six and Seven provide vivid examples of curriculum integration through Mantle of the Expert. Chapter Four shows how teachers challenged a class of Years 5/6 children to grapple with ethical issues related to animal rights. Working in the role of expert researchers, children were encouraged to explore different and contrasting perspectives on the issue of feral horses in the Kaimanawa region. Through a gradual process of unfolding tensions and interactions with fictional characters, the children were exposed to the contradictory views of a protest group, Wild and Free, who were opposed to the culling of horses, and the Department of Conservation, who wished to protect the native flora and fauna threatened by the horses. This chapter describes the ongoing planning process undertaken by teachers, the sequence of activities experienced by the children and the learning that arose across the curriculum.

In Chapter Five the context for learning in a Years 5/6 class was the Stone Age, and Mantle of the Expert formed the main approach to the inquiry. The company the class formed was named, by class vote, Realistic Artists and Performers. The issue the company faced was to create an interactive museum for children that educated them about living in Stone Age times. This purpose was the catalyst for a range of interactive activities, which the children developed, trialled and refined. The culmination of the unit was the invitation to a Year 4 class to participate as museum visitors, giving this fictional company a real audience. Feedback from the Years 5/6 children revealed their learning gains and their advice to adults on what makes for engaging learning.

Chapter Six outlines two integrated units drawing on a syndicate camp experience in the Waitomo area. A range of learning experiences included cultural and physical histories, fossils, caving and a visit to the Waitomo Education Centre. This was a catalyst for subsequent learning at school in the fields of science, art, drama, ICT and English. The challenge was for the Years 5/6 classes to consider both the preservation of the environment and the education of present and future generations. Complicating this was the necessity to take seriously the issues surrounding preservation of natural caves and the contrasting needs of a mining company. These tensions and contrasting viewpoints were a major aspect of the study and spearheaded the need to deepen investigation.

Chapter Seven describes a unit of work taught in a Year 3 class. Using a children's story as a starting point, the teacher guided the children through an exploration of the Māori concept of mauri (life force) and the environmental and social impacts of people on New Zealand's landscape. Using the Mantle of the Expert approach, children worked in role as expert archaeologists charged with researching the history of a (fictional) piece of land. The chapter outlines the ways in which teaching in role and symbols were used in this unit. It also details the learning activities carried out, which included social history, creative writing, report writing and art making in clay and other media. A focus of discussion in this case study is the conjunction between the spiritual basis and ethos of the school (a special character Catholic primary school) and the teacher's own Māori heritage.

Chapter Eight departs from the Mantle of the Expert approach and places the focus on visual art-inspired integration. The chapter shows how an arson event triggered a whole-school inquiry centred on children's perspectives of how to rebuild and renew their damaged school. Negotiation became an essential element of the rebuilding process. Children, teachers and community members combined skills and expertise to plan and implement an arts-based transformation of the school grounds. This collaborative process served to restore a sense of community and ensure communal guardianship of the school environment.

Chapter Nine provides an example of curriculum integration where the teacher and her Year 3 children collaboratively investigated the needs of a Samoan school devastated by a tsunami. The project spanned a whole school term and included a vast array of community support and involvement. The children drew upon a range of learning areas and key competencies within the authentic context of the extensive aid project. In effect, this integrated project reflects the curriculum goal of children as "active seekers, users and creators of knowledge" (Ministry of Education, 2007, p. 8). It also provides an example of promoting children's agency through socially responsive activism. The challenges, processes and outcomes of the project are briefly outlined and the significance for teachers is discussed.

The overarching purpose of the unit outlined in Chapter Ten is to help Year 3 children sharpen their writing through poetry and enhance their visual art skills. Poetry, when taught well, helps children carefully select and control the format and use of vivid vocabulary. This discipline of choosing the best possible words in the "right" order to form a pleasing structure is very pertinent at this level. Teachers know that many Year 3 children tend to ramble at length with their new-found powers of written expression. This can lead to lengthy narratives that serve little purpose and lack audience appeal.

The integrated aspect of this unit was deliberately focused on visual art to complement the poetic writing. The teacher found that this connection between visual art and the poetic has considerable merit in terms of producing high-quality work and a sense of pride in the children as both artists and writers. As with the poetic writing, the emphasis on visual art is intended to sharpen their focus and help them look more closely (Eisner, 2000). Through visual art the focus is placed on the children's artistic skills and their ability to interpret through visual modes what they see. Looking carefully, sketching, focusing, painting and collage are all deliberate acts that help deepen children's perceptual skills.

The final chapter pulls together the themes emerging across the previous chapters. It raises issues, discusses findings from the project, considers ramifications for practice and suggests implications for further research.

Each chapter about classroom practice is structured using a common format, to help the reader. First, the context is described by way of an *introduction*. This includes the nature of the school and the class level. Second, the *big idea* underpinning the integrated unit is described. Third, *the hook* that is employed to engage students' interest in the unit is outlined. This is followed by a section on *organising for learning*, which enables readers to see how teachers managed the logistics of the unit. The fifth section, *deepening learning*, shows how an integrated curriculum fosters students' ability to seek and create knowledge. The next section lists the *curriculum links* emanating from each unit so that readers can see what achievement objectives were covered. Finally, each chapter draws a *conclusion* about the significance of the unit described.

This seven-part structure provides a guide for readers so that they appreciate the order within the complexity. It also offers a scaffold for teachers wanting to try units of their own.

Conclusion

Many New Zealand teachers are adept at picking out the best parts of research findings in education and bringing their own home-grown creative intelligence to the table in order to develop programmes that are uniquely theirs and of world-class standard. We encourage readers to do just that with this book. As this introduction notes, our national character is such that we have a spirit of creativity, flair and innovation. This spirit should be celebrated and encouraged in education among teachers and students alike. If this book in any way kindles teachers' creativity and reignites their passion for integration, then we have achieved what we hoped. If nothing else, this book is a reminder to hard-working, creative, talented teachers who negotiate the curriculum with their students that they are not alone, and that they should be proud of what they achieve.

Fig 1.5 *Year 0 child's paint and pastel chook*

References

Beane, J. (2005). *A reason to teach: Creating classrooms of dignity and hope.* Portsmouth, NH: Heinemann.

Bolstad, R. (2010). *The contributions of learning in the arts to educational, social and economic outcomes: Part 1—A review of the literature.* Wellington: Ministry of Culture and Heritage.

Bolstad, R. (2011). *The contributions of learning in the arts to educational, social and economic outcomes: Part 2—A literature synthesis.* Wellington: Ministry of Culture and Heritage.

Brough, C. (2008). Student-centred curriculum integration in action: "I was wondering if you could tell me how much one meat patty and one sausage costs?" *set: Research Information for Teachers, 3,* 9–14.

Charmaz, K. (1995). Grounded theory. In J. A. Smith, R. Harre, & L. V. Langenhove (Eds.), *Rethinking methods in psychology* (pp. 27–49). London: Sage.

Charmaz, K. (2005). Grounded theory in the 21st century: Applications for advancing social justice studies. In N. K. Denzin & Y. S. Lincoln (Eds.), *The Sage handbook of qualitative research* (3rd ed., pp. 507–536). Thousand Oaks, CA: Sage.

Chicago Arts Partnerships in Education. (2009). *Research and evaluation series: Contributions to arts and learning.* Retrieved from http://www.capeweb.org/rcurrent.html

Creswell, J. W. (2005). *Educational research: Planning, conducting and evaluating quantitative and qualitative research* (2nd ed.). Upper Saddle River, NJ: Pearson Education.

Department of Education. (1937). *Syllabus of instruction for public schools.* Wellington: Government Printer.

Dowden, R. A. (2006). *Curriculum integration for early adolescent schooling in Aotearoa New Zealand: Worthy of serious trial?* Unpublished doctoral thesis, Massey University, Palmerston North.

Efland, A. (2002). *Art and cognition: Integrating the visual arts in the curriculum.* New York: Teachers College Press.

Eisner, E. (2000, January). Ten lessons the arts teach: Learning and the arts: Crossing boundaries. *Proceedings from an invitational meeting for education, arts and youth funders* (pp. 7–14). Los Angeles.

Engel, S. (2011). Children's need to know: Curiosity in schools. *Harvard Educational Review, 81*(4), 625–645.

Ewing, R., & Simons, J. (2004). *Beyond the script: Drama in the classroom take two.* Newtown, NSW: PETA.

Fraser, D. (2000). Curriculum integration: What it is and is not. *set: Research Information for Teachers, 3,* 34–37.

Fraser, D., Henderson, C., Price, G., Bevege, F., Gilbert, G., Goodman, A. et al. (2006). *The art of the matter: The development and extension of ways of knowing in the arts.* Teaching and Learning Research Initiative Final Project Report. Wellington: NZCER Press.

Gibson, R., & Ewing, R. (2011). *Transforming the curriculum through the arts.* South Yarra, VIC: Palgrave Macmillan.

Jacobs, H. H. (2004). *Getting results with curriculum mapping.* Alexandria, VA: Association for Supervision and Curriculum Development.

Jones, A., & Middleton, S. (Eds.). (2009). *The kiss and the ghost: Sylvia Ashton-Warner and New Zealand.* Wellington: NZCER Press.

Lowe, R. (2007). *The death of progressive education: How teachers lost control of the classroom.* London: Routledge.

Ministry of Education. (2007). *The New Zealand curriculum.* Wellington: Learning Media.

Nuthall, G. (2001, December). *The cultural myths and realities of teaching and learning.* Paper presented at the New Zealand Association for Research in Education conference, Christchurch.

Nuthall, G. (2007). *The hidden lives of learners.* Wellington: NCZER Press.

Richardson, E. (1972). *In the early world* (2nd ed.). Wellington: New Zealand Council for Educational Research.

Richardson, E. (2012). *In the early world* (3rd ed.). Wellington: NZCER Press.

CHAPTER TWO

Curriculum Integration

Deborah Fraser

Introduction

One of the guiding principles of the curriculum is coherence, whereby students are offered "a broad education that makes links within and across learning areas" (Ministry of Education, 2007, p. 9). When used effectively, curriculum integration provides a learning environment that offers this coherent education, allowing connections to be made within and across subjects (Beane, 1997; Etim, 2005; Fraser, 2000; Murdoch & Hornsby, 1997). As Drake (1998) argues:

> The world we are living in is changing, and education must change with it. If we live in an interconnected and interdependent world, it only makes sense that knowledge be presented as interconnected and interdependent. (p. 24)

Nonetheless, it could be argued that curriculum integration remains one of the most confused topics in education today. Many teachers and researchers use the term to mean a variety of things, some of which have nothing to do with curriculum integration. The confusions surrounding the term have undoubtedly hindered consistent professional development and research in this area.

Curriculum integration is a design that supports the need for learners to be actively involved in their learning, through being part of the decision-making process (Dowden, 2006; Drake, 1998; Etim, 2005; Fraser & Charteris, 1998; Whyte & Strang, 1998). While many discuss the benefits of curriculum integration, this design still remains largely misunderstood due to the number of varying definitions available and the confusion between this approach and others (Fraser, 2000; Mathews & Cleary, 1993; Murdoch & Hamston, 1999).

What does curriculum integration mean?

Current talk about curriculum integration is almost completely ahistorical, suggesting alternately that it is rooted in reforms of the 1960s or that it is a recent 'fad' that began in the late 1980s. Furthermore, the same current talk almost always implies that curriculum integration is simply a matter of rearranging lesson plans as overlaps among subject areas are identified. Neither interpretation is true, of course, but the fact that both are widely believed has seriously limited discussions about curriculum integration and the scope of its use in schools (Beane, 1997, p. 4).

One of the best ways to understand curriculum integration is to discuss what it is not. First, it is not ahistorical, as Beane rightly points out. The roots of curriculum integration are to be found in the progressive education movement of the early 1900s and are evident in the work of Dewey (1910, 1913), Kilpatrick (1926) and others. Dewey (1902) stated that within the curriculum, "facts are torn away from their original place in experience and rearranged with reference to some general principle" (p. 6). This concern highlights the need for education to be realistic and relevant to the students' world, calling upon their prior knowledge and experiences in broadening their understanding (Mathews & Cleary, 1993; Whyte & Strang, 1998).

Curriculum integration is responsive to this concern because it values the students' prior knowledge and uses this as an initial starting point to be built upon (Beane, 1997; Brough, 2007; Dowden, 2006; Mathews & Cleary, 1993). This is an active process that makes learning relevant to what the students already know (Boomer, Lester, Oncore, & Cook, 1992). In order to illustrate what curriculum integration is, Pring (2006) employs a metaphor, arguing that it depicts "the seamless coat of learning", whereby subjects are viewed as interconnected rather than isolated from one another. This notion is reflected in the Ministry of Education's (2007) assertion that "all learning should make use of the natural connections that exist between learning areas", as each individual area is "valuable for the pathways it opens to other learning" (p. 16).

Second, curriculum integration is not what teachers did in the 1960s and 1970s; it is not "centre of interest"-based teaching, nor is it purely child-centred teaching. In fact the tendency for people to claim it is totally student driven does teachers a disservice. Teachers have considerable curriculum knowledge and pedagogical skills that ensure that curriculum integration provides a challenging and rewarding learning environment. The chapters that follow in this book underline teachers' role in negotiating curriculum with their students, not relinquishing all direction and control to them. Moreover, the chapters provide a variety of examples along a continuum of curriculum integration. Some show the teacher as centrally involved in a leading role throughout much of the process, while others reveal students taking increasing responsibility for how the curriculum is enacted. Even within the more teacher-directed examples to follow however, there are multiple opportunities for students to negotiate the "what" and "how" of their learning. So while the teacher's role may vary in the chapters to follow, the emphasis on negotiation remains important.

Finally, curriculum integration is not the teaching of thematic units, whereby a central topic forms the "theme", with each curriculum area explored for its potential to contribute to that theme. This third point creates the most common confusion and has sparked the most debate. It is worth examining why this is the case.

Different interpretations: Thematic units vs curriculum integration

The term "curriculum integration" has frequently been used as a synonym for thematic units (often called "multidisciplinary approaches" overseas). However, thematic units are distinctly different. Some would argue that thematic units are part of the continuum of curriculum integration and are an important starting point, but this is not always the case. Thematic units, for all the fun and interest they can promote, are not curriculum integration and may stop teachers from developing pedagogy that fosters curriculum integration.

How do thematic units differ from curriculum integration?

- Curriculum integration involves students in negotiating the curriculum with their teacher. This may start rather modestly, with students suggesting activities within a study, or be more substantial, such as students taking a role in co-planning, exploring and evaluating a study.

- Curriculum integration tends to be issues driven rather than topic driven. In the chapters to follow a number of issues are threaded throughout. These include ethical dilemmas, weighing up evidence and argument, exploring ways to preserve the past and educate for the present, making museums more interesting for children, rebuilding a school environment and instigating an aid project. Where topics are evident, these are regarded as a means to an end, not an end in itself. For example, the topic of living in Stone Age times features in Chapter Five, but the issue of how to make museums (and thus learning) enticing for children is one of the main issues explored.
- Curriculum integration involves the teacher scaffolding students' learning rather than directing them. This scaffolding is the sophisticated artistry of teachers' work—work that is far more nuanced, intuitive and skilful than mere telling. It requires that teachers know when to intervene and when to hold back. It also requires an innate sense of just how to intervene. The best response might be a well-placed question or a statement that conveys curiosity. There is still a place, of course, for direct teaching. However, within parameters there are frequent opportunities for students' agency, with freedom to experiment and initiate.
- Finally, curriculum integration only draws upon learning areas that relate to the central issues of the inquiry. No attempt is made to cover all curriculum areas. Instead, the learning areas drawn upon are those that are germane to the study and naturally arise from the inquiry. This means that the teacher cannot fully plan in advance, as the learning areas that students will engage in are not always known at the outset, and the issues-oriented focus requires an openness to what unfolds rather than prescribing what will be.

Thematic units differ in a number of ways.

- Thematic units focus on a particular topic chosen by the teacher, such as the Middle Ages, dinosaurs, sea mammals or plastics.

The topic itself is the main focus. This largely reflects a model of learning where the aim is for students to obtain information about the topic.

- Thematic units attempt to cover the curriculum. For example, the teacher-chosen topic is considered through the lens of each learning area as teachers plan how each could contribute to an exploration of the theme. Teachers might use a web diagram to plan the unit and often brainstorm in syndicates a number of ingenious activities. For example, in a study of the Middle Ages, students may build a castle in their room (technology), perform a play (drama), develop an alternative currency (mathematics), locate and perform medieval songs (music) and examine the role of guilds in the period (social studies). Achievement objectives are considered within each learning area and assessment decisions are made. Students are often encouraged to bring materials to school that would support the theme.

- Thematic units involve the teacher in planning and directing students in activities, which means the teacher can be fully planned in advance and recycle units from year to year.

Any approach to curriculum can be implemented poorly or executed well. For instance, there can be well-designed thematic units that foster learning, just as there can be poor attempts at curriculum integration. The converse is also the case. The teacher remains the crucial factor. However, curriculum integration affords students status as negotiators in the pursuit of knowledge. Their say matters and, as a result, their commitment is enhanced:

> Out of negotiation comes a sense of ownership in learners for the work they are to do and therefore a commitment to it. Learning is an active process. Teachers can't do it for learners. Information may be imposed but understanding cannot be for it must come from within. Students learn best when they want to. They want to when they are doing it for themselves, as a result of their own needs. (Cook, 1992, p. 16)

A common misapprehension is that teachers have little say within curriculum integration. However, the process of negotiation means that teachers have considerable input, and there are times when they will direct and lead. But they also involve, invite and expect the students' contributions, and these contributions are taken seriously.

This process does not just happen, and teachers need to scaffold students' ideas and skills throughout. This is where teachers' pedagogical abilities are fully employed and crucial to the success of the approach. In effect, the investigative process is negotiated between teachers and students and reflects how research occurs in the world at large. In many ways the curriculum integration process is parallel to the one taken by research students at university level. In negotiation with their supervisors, they identify an area of concern and raise some related questions. They investigate what is already known about the area (a literature review), and consider ways to examine the problems identified. They may collect data in the field, interview people, make comparisons and trial interventions. They may then refine their interventions or create graphs of their results, make inferences, build analysis and identify themes, which they then discuss, drawing some conclusions. Their conclusions are compared with what was previously known and implications for further study or learning are indicated. At every step they gain feedback and guidance from their supervisors on the skills required and the development of ideas, as well as the expression of those ideas.

This is very much the process that students in classrooms undertake, with their teachers as "supervisors", providing the necessary teaching and guidance during curriculum integration. Although 5-year-olds would not undertake a review of the literature, they would be part of a class discussion on what is already known about the topic and what they would like to know more about. In addition, the teacher will be assessing what skills the students need in order to pursue the questions and concerns that are generated.

In the above explanation, curriculum integration actively involves students, using problems and issues of importance to them in developing a curriculum that goes beyond the confines of stand-alone subjects. However, Murdoch and Hornsby (1997) caution that curriculum integration "does not do away with the distinctions between those subjects or learning areas—these remain important for the purposes of balance and organisation" (p. 1). This salient point is important to underline. Curriculum integration draws on the distinct knowledge of learning areas in ways that preserve the integrity of those areas. The chapters that follow provide a number of examples of what this looks like in practice.

Virtue, Wilson and Ingram (2009) express the concern that teachers transitioning from a thematic approach to a fully integrated approach are likely to encounter many challenges, because experience in cross-curriculum planning and negotiating with students is necessary for the approach to be successful. As mentioned previously, curriculum integration involves students in decisions about the direction and content of learning (Beane, 1997; Beane, 2005; Boomer et al., 1992; Brough, 2007; Fraser & Charteris, 1998; Mathews & Cleary, 1993; Murdoch & Hornsby, 1997). Thematic units, however, tend to be decided on and planned by the teacher, with very little if any, input from the students (Fraser & Charteris, 1998; Jacobs, 1993; Mathews & Cleary, 1993). In this sense, the teacher is an activity provider, planning exercises that may foster student engagement, but also limiting students' ownership and learning (Beane, 1997; Fraser & Charteris, 1998).

There are various possible reasons for the popularity and longevity of thematic units. The teacher can plan in advance and collect activities over time. This decreases time spent on preparation in the long run, as themes can be recycled in subsequent years with just minor updates. Syndicates can pool resources, which further increases efficiency in busy teachers' lives. Assessment can be designed to match the activities, and a sense of curriculum coverage, albeit thin, is achieved. There is also the "feel good" factor when a class is "doing" dinosaurs, immersed in a series of tenuously connected but engaging activities around an appealing topic. Champions of thematic approaches, however, fail to interrogate the "dubious educational value ... or the lack of rationale" (Dowden, 2006, p. 184) of such designs.

Within the two approaches the role of the teacher is also considerably different, because thematic units are largely teacher directed whereas curriculum integration involves the teacher less as director and more as negotiator with students (Boomer et al., 1992; Brough, 2007; Drake, 1998; Fraser & Charteris, 1998). One area where these two approaches appear to be similar is in the connections they both make between learning areas. However, the manner in which these connections are made is different. In thematic units, subjects are placed at the centre and the curriculum design "forces a fit" across the curriculum. In curriculum integration, issues form the centre, and learning areas are drawn upon when required.

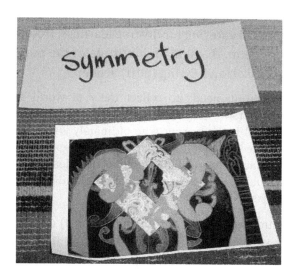

Fig 2.1 *Maths and art*

The role of negotiation

Negotiating curriculum with students forms the core of curriculum integration pedagogy (see, for example, Beane; 1997; Beane, Ellsworth, & Miller, 1996; Boomer et al., 1992; Brodhagen, 1995). Negotiating curriculum is also valued for the culturally responsive and inclusive learning environment it creates (Bishop & Berryman, 2009; Brough, 2007; Fraser & Paraha, 2002). This negotiation can include involving students in planning, decision-making and assessment processes (Boomer et al., 1992; Brough, 2007). Negotiating curriculum has been included by Bishop and Berryman (2009) as a key strategy in the Effective Teaching Profile, because it has been recognised as an approach that caters for the learning needs of Māori students in secondary schools. They reveal that negotiating curriculum makes learning interesting for the students because it views them as capable and agentic, enabling them to contribute to what and how they learn (Bishop & Berryman, 2009). In doing so, student ownership of the learning is gained, which fosters enthusiasm and enhances student motivation (Boomer et al., 1992).

Drake (1998) claims that with curriculum negotiation of this kind, genuine connections are made between the students' world, the classroom and the issues of importance to them. Others, such as Brough (2007), also assert its usefulness in catering for diverse learners. However, as with any approach to curriculum, the skill and attitude of the teacher remain the crucial factor. As Gibson and Ewing (2011) argue:

> Curriculum integration needs to reflect the real world and therefore be interactive. As teachers we must remember that if we believe in a constructivist theory of learning, it is the learner who ultimately will do the integrating by building knowledge and relating it to his or her existing understandings. Nevertheless we have a responsibility to construct learning experiences that are both intellectually and creatively demanding, and scaffold the knowledge integrating processes of our students. (p. 33)

A longitudinal study by Bishop and Brinegar (2011) of students at middle school found that students themselves can initially resist curriculum integration, conveying attitudes of scepticism and indifference. However, even in the early stages a number of students recognised that curriculum integration afforded them a greater say in what happened in the classroom, plus the opportunity to present to audiences. Over subsequent years, regard for the approach grew, with students reflecting on the learning gains made from integrated projects.

Challenges

Curriculum integration requires a shift in the traditional role of the teacher. It is more dynamic, interactive and finely nuanced than teaching a thematic unit. It requires teachers to share decision making and the messy process of inquiry, where the outcomes are unknown. As such, it can feel both demanding and daunting for those who are new to it. Drake (1998) comments on teachers' feelings of exhaustion when trying curriculum integration because they are required to take on roles different from their usual ways of operating. Some teachers may feel threatened by this approach for a number of reasons, including their reluctance to share decision making and their preference for having activities carefully planned well ahead of time (Etim, 2005; Fraser & Charteris, 1998).

Fig 2.2 *Girls searching for relevant information online*

A further challenge that is known to cause concern is teachers' lack of knowledge about curriculum integration. When not done well, curriculum integration can become as forced or artificial as any poorly executed approach, resulting in lack of student motivation and engagement (Beane, 2005; Jacobs, 1993; Murdoch & Hamston, 1999). Another impediment for some is the concern that they will not be covering what the curriculum requires. Teachers do need to remember the big picture and ensure their music programme, for instance, is not overlooked just because music does not feature in an integrated unit. There is place and space for stand-alone subject teaching alongside any integrated unit. The erroneous belief that curriculum integration incorporates all learning areas leads some to raise this concern. Curriculum integration only draws on those learning areas germane to the inquiry at hand.

Fig 2.3 *Year 5/6 children identifying cross-curricula connections*

27

There is no doubt that schooling is becoming more high stakes with the drive for collecting and reporting data on achievement in literacy and numeracy. This increased emphasis on two learning areas affects teachers' planning and curriculum decision making. It narrows what counts as knowledge in schools, with accountability mechanisms in place to ensure this restricted focus is maintained. As a result, teachers may feel that integrating curriculum detracts from the main business of their work. However, Drake (1998) and Drake and Burns (2004) provide numerous ways to meet standards and enhance student learning, through integration.

Finally, time is one of the biggest factors in the successful implementation of curriculum integration, and some believe that curriculum integration requires more time than what is readily available in the classroom schedule (Boomer et al., 1992; Murdoch & Hornsby, 1997). Time, however, is a perennial challenge in any approach to teaching and it should not be used as an excuse not to innovate. Anecdotal evidence suggests that teachers save time in the long run because they are not caught up in the minutiae of narrow planning, teaching and assessing, but are instead liberated to facilitate students' inquiry into deep and compelling issues. Instead of curriculum coverage, the emphasis is on depth of learning.

Implications

When teachers employ curriculum integration, Beane (1997) claims that relationships are strengthened and power dynamics are challenged in the process. Collaborative skills are enhanced through having a collective focus on inquiry. This encourages teachers and students to work alongside one another (Beane, 1997; Drake, 1998; Etim, 2005). Some studies claim that students' levels of engagement and persistence are greatly enhanced because curriculum integration personally involves the students in their own learning (Drake, 1998; Fraser, 2000; Murdoch & Hamston, 1999; Paterson, 2003). Further benefits mentioned are fewer attendance concerns, less disruptive behaviour and fewer discipline problems (Drake, 1998; Paterson, 2003).

An additional benefit for students is that, through learning in an integrative fashion, they become better prepared for life through examining social issues of personal significance (Beane, 1997, 2005; Drake, 1998; Etim, 2005; Wineburg & Grossman, 2000). Reflective and critical thinking skills are developed as students make connections between school activities and their own life experiences (Bishop & Berryman, 2009; Drake, 1998; Etim, 2005; Fraser & Charteris, 1998; Murdoch & Hamston, 1999).

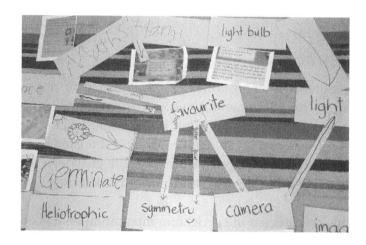

Fig 2.4 *Cross-curricula connections by Year 3 children*

Teachers who have made the effort to understand curriculum integration, challenge their existing practices and negotiate curriculum with students have found they are more than compensated by their students' learning progress. This growth includes high motivation, depth of learning and persistence. Some of the specific changes in their students that teachers have reported include the following (Fraser & Whyte, 1999, pp. 1–2):

> My kids didn't want to see the slides at the zoo [which the zoo officer had prepared for school trips] they wanted to keep asking her questions. (Junior class teacher)

> The learning activities are more spontaneous, driven by children in their search for answers about their world. (Middle primary teacher)

> The children don't need to satisfy the teacher as much as they used to. They gain pleasure out of reaching their own aims. (Junior class teacher)

> I was really surprised by the range of questions they came up with. (Teacher of 5- and 6-year-olds)

The children are more returning to things, like the greenhouse effect, and revisiting it at a deeper level. They're using the ideas they developed earlier in the year to set up experiments and extend their knowledge later in the year. They never used to do that. (Middle primary teacher)

I've been so impressed by the quality of the children's writing and discussions... now they comment on each other's ideas back and forth. (Middle primary teacher)

Conclusion

Improving students' learning is inextricably linked to the improvement of teaching (e.g., Darling-Hammond, 1998). Curriculum integration promotes a "high" pedagogy (Beane, 1997) that is culturally responsive, relevant and engaging (Bishop & Glynn, 1999). The skill, knowledge and passion required for such a pedagogy is a considerable challenge for teachers, but one that many welcome when they realise the learning gains for their students.

Unpacking the process of curriculum integration enables teachers to understand the crucial details and the depth of learning and teaching. Many will see the strong links between this approach and inquiry-based learning. These processes bring teachers closer to how students learn and how much they *can* learn. Curriculum integration also enables teachers to understand what students want to learn, and therefore what they *need* to learn to access the knowledge they desire.

It seems clear that the benefits of curriculum integration and the learning experience it provides far outweigh the challenges and concerns related to its implementation. In terms of further research, it would be beneficial to know more about the learning gains for students who are experiencing an integrated curriculum. This book goes some way towards providing tangible data from classroom research that reveals what that learning looks like.

The case studies of classroom practice in this book reveal a range of examples that connect curriculum. Some (such as Chapter Nine) clearly exemplify the intent of curriculum integration as described above. Others reflect some curriculum integration principles but are not as far along the continuum. A few thematic elements are evident in several chapters, such as some teacher planned and directed activities within a partly negotiated unit. We hope that this variation is helpful for readers as they consider their own practice and reflect upon where they "sit" on the curriculum integration continuum. Readers may also like to consider the opportunities for negotiation outlined in each chapter.

Each of the chapters has in common: the importance of sharing decision making at various points with students; an emphasis on student engagement in solving problems (not just following instructions); and units where the focus is confined to a few learning areas rather than stretching to cover the curriculum. In summary, the case studies in this book show effective ways to connect curriculum, negotiate with students and deepen the learning experience.

Acknowledgements

This chapter is a revised and updated version of an earlier article: Fraser, D. (2000). Curriculum integration: What it is and is not. *set: Research Information for Teachers*, *3*, 34–37 (reprinted with permission). Sacha Davey is acknowledged for reviewing some of the additional literature cited.

References

Beane, J. A. (1997) *Curriculum integration: Designing the core of democratic education.* New York: Teachers College Press.

Beane, J. A. (2005). *A reason to teach: Creating classrooms of dignity and hope.* Portsmouth, NH: Heinemann.

Beane, J. A., Ellsworth, E. A., & Miller, J. L. (Producers). (1996). *Doing curriculum integration* [video]. Available from Wisconsin Department of Public Instruction, Drawer 179, Milwaukee, WI, 53293-0179.

Bishop, P. A., & Brinegar, K. (2011). Student learning and engagement in the context of curriculum integration. *Middle Grades Research Journal*, *6*(4), 207–220.

Bishop, R., & Berryman, M. (2009). The Te Kotahitanga effective teaching profile. *set: Research Information for Teachers*, *2*, 27–34.

Bishop, R., & Glynn, T. (1999). *Culture counts: Changing power relations in education.* Palmerston North: Dunmore Press.

Boomer, G., Lester, N., Oncore, C., & Cook, J. (Eds.). (1992). *Negotiating the curriculum: Education for the 21st century.* London, UK: Falmer Press.

Brodhagen, B. (1995). The situation made us special. In M. Apple & J. Beane (Eds.), *Democratic schools* (pp. 83–100). Alexandria, VA: Association for Supervision and Curriculum Development.

Brough, C. (2007). Nurturing talent through curriculum integration. *Kairaranga, 8*(1), 8–12.

Cook, J. (1992). Negotiating the curriculum: Programming for learning. In G. Boomer, N. Lester, C. Onore, & J. Cook (Eds.), *Negotiating the curriculum: Educating for the 21st century* (pp. 15–31). London: Falmer Press.

Darling-Hammond, L. (1998). Teachers and teaching: Testing hypotheses from a National Commission report. *Educational Researcher, 27*(1), 5–15.

Dewey, J. (1902). *Child and the curriculum.* Chicago, IL: University of Chicago Press.

Dewey, J. (1910). *How we think.* Boston, MA: Heath.

Dewey, J. (1913). *Interest and effort in education.* Boston, MA: Houghton Mifflin.

Dowden, R. A. (2006). *Curriculum integration for early adolescent schooling in Aotearoa New Zealand: Worthy of serious trial?* Unpublished doctoral thesis, Massey University, Palmerston North.

Drake, S. M. (1998). *Creating integrated curriculum: Proven ways to increase student learning.* Thousand Oaks, CA: Corwin Press.

Drake, S. M., & Burns, R. C. (2004). *Meeting standards through integrated curriculum.* Alexandria, VA: Association for Supervision and Curriculum Development.

Etim, J. S. (2005). *Curriculum integration K-12: Theory and practice.* Lanham, MD: University Press of America.

Fraser, D. (2000). Curriculum integration: What it is and is not. *set: Research Information for Teachers, 3*, 34–37.

Fraser, D., & Charteris, C. (1998, October). *What is curriculum integration and why do teachers need to know?* Paper presented at the New Zealand Teacher Education conference, Hamilton.

Fraser, D., & Paraha, H. (2002). Curriculum integration as treaty praxis. *Waikato Journal of Education, 8*, 57–70.

Fraser, D., & Whyte, B. (1999). *Curriculum integration: Milestone report four.* Wellington: Ministry of Education.

Gibson, R., & Ewing, R. (2011). *Transforming the curriculum through the arts.* South Yarra, VIC: Palgrave Macmillan.

Jacobs, H. H. (1993). Mathematics integration: A common-sense approach to curriculum development. *Arithmetic Teacher, 40*(6), 301–302.

Kilpatrick, W. (1926). *Education for a changing civilization.* New York: Macmillan.

Mathews, B., & Cleary, P. (1993). *The integrated curriculum in use: Practical ideas for planning and assessment.* Auckland: Ashton Scholastic.

Ministry of Education. (2007). *The New Zealand curriculum.* Wellington: Learning Media.

Murdoch, K., & Hamston, J. (1999). *Knowing me, knowing you: Exploring identity and difference through an integrated curriculum.* Burwood, VIC: Dellasta Publishing.

Murdoch, K., & Hornsby, D. (1997). *Planning curriculum connections: Whole-school planning for integrated curriculum.* South Yarra, VIC: Eleanor Curtain Publishing.

Paterson, J. (2003). Curriculum integration in a standards-based world. *Middleground: The Magazine of Middle Education, 7*(1), 10–12.

Pring, R. (2006). Curriculum integration. *Journal of Philosophy of Education, 5*(2), 170–200.

Virtue, D. C., Wilson, J. L., & Ingram, N. (2009). L.E.S.S can be more! *Middle School Journal, 40*(3), 4–11.

Whyte, B., & Strang, P. (1998, October). *Implications of curriculum integration for professional development of teachers.* Paper presented at the New Zealand Teacher Education conference, Hamilton.

Wineburg, S., & Grossman, P. (Eds.). (2000). *Interdisciplinary curriculum: Challenges to implementation.* Columbia University, NY, & London, UK: Teachers College Press.

CHAPTER THREE

Dorothy Heathcote's Mantle of the Expert Approach to Teaching and Learning: A Brief Introduction

Viv Aitken

Introduction

In four of the case studies described in this book, teachers opted to teach using the dramatic inquiry teaching approach known as Mantle of the Expert. It is the aim of this chapter to provide the reader with further background information about this approach, including its core principles, impacts on learning and place in the New Zealand educational context. Of course it will only be possible to offer the briefest of summaries here. For fuller description and discussion, please refer to Dorothy Heathcote and Gavin Bolton's *Drama for Learning* (Heathcote & Bolton, 1994). Also useful are Sandra Heston's very thorough PhD study, available online at http://www.partnership.mmu.ac.uk, the numerous articles and materials available at http://www.mantleoftheexpert.com and Bolton's excellent biography of Heathcote's life, which describes how the approach developed (Bolton, 2003).

The Mantle of the Expert approach was developed by UK-based drama educator Dorothy Heathcote (1926–2012). It was the culmination of over 40 years of practice, which saw Heathcote lauded as "one of the greatest teachers of the twentieth century" (John Carroll, cited in Heston, 1993, p. 1). Heathcote saw Mantle of the Expert as a "clear system" with "operant laws", which she defined and explained through numerous charts and addresses over the years (see http://www.mantleoftheexpert.com; Heston, 1993). At the same time, Heathcote always acknowledged that the approach had enormous complexity and fluidity, and she considered herself to be learning, uncovering and discovering new aspects right to the end of her life (Heathcote, 2009). Heathcote's work has been further developed and theorised by academics and practitioners around the world, including Brian Edmiston (Edmiston, 2003), Luke Abbott (Abbott, 2007), John Carroll (Carroll, Anderson, & Cameron, 2006), Stig Erikkson (Erikkson, 2011) and others.

The metaphor of the mantle: The child at the centre

The name "Mantle of the Expert" evokes the idea of learning growing like a mantle, or cloak, surrounding the learner. In some ways the image resonates with the concept of the Māori korowai, or feathered cloak, which is bestowed as a sign of mana, or respect, knowledge and status. However, Heathcote makes it clear that unlike the korowai, the "mantle" in Mantle of the Expert is not a garment to be gifted by another, but a quality that grows from within:

> Mantle is not a cloak by which a person is recognised. This is no garment to cover. I use it as a *quality*: of leadership, carrying standards of behaviour, morality, responsibility, ethics and the spiritual basis of all action. The mantle embodies the standards I ascribe to. It grows by usage, not garment stitching. (Heathcote, 2009, pp. 1–2)

As Heathcote's words imply, the Mantle of the Expert approach places the child at the centre of the learning. The teacher's role is to create the conditions whereby a mantle of leadership, knowledge, competency and understanding grows around the child. This approach assumes a progressive view of learning, responsive to the needs of the child (Heston, 1993). The child centrism begins in the planning stages, with the teacher starting from the children's interests and needs, alongside the curriculum objectives, and continues in the classroom interactions, where the teacher consciously positions the children as competent co-constructors of the learning. Although placing the child at the centre, and including strong elements of inquiry, the approach is far from child-led. The role played by the teacher, both in and outside the drama, is a crucial part of the success of Mantle of the Expert.

Broadly speaking, Mantle of the Expert draws on three teaching modalities: inquiry learning; drama for learning (closely related to drama-in-education, or, as it is sometimes called, process drama); and what we might call "expert framing", which involves children being positioned as adult experts. This reframing asks the children to "frame" or think about their learning in a new way. It also involves a conscious repositioning of power within the teacher–student relationship. Abbott suggests that for Mantle of the Expert to work at its best, the teacher needs to be conscious of, and adept in, all three of these modes of teaching (2007, pp. 3, 23).

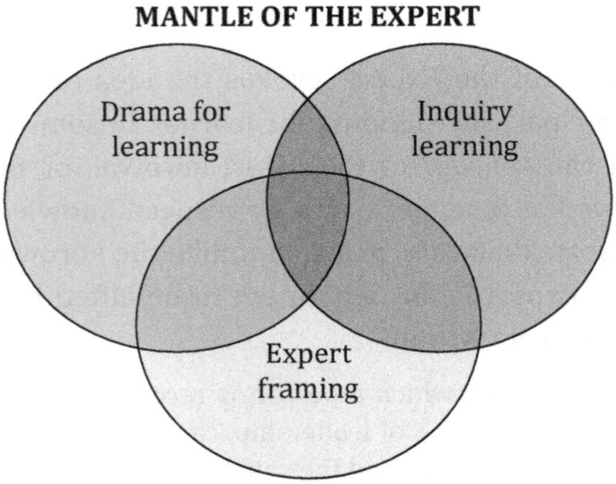

MANTLE OF THE EXPERT

Figure 3.1 *The three pedagogic structures of Mantle of the Expert*
Source: Adapted from Abbott (2007)

In our research project we found that teachers using Mantle of the Expert had different strengths depending on their prior teaching experience. For teachers with a background in inquiry learning it was often the drama for learning aspects that challenged them, while those familiar with process drama often needed to build skills in guiding student-led inquiry. As for the third of these modalities—the systems and strategies that comprise the building of the expert frame—these were a new challenge for all involved, and they are the main focus of discussion in this chapter.

Core components of the approach

Overview

So, what does Mantle of the Expert look like in practice? Although each Mantle of the Expert experience is unique, there are certain core components, as italicised in the following description. In its very simplest terms, Mantle of the Expert is about teachers and children taking on *roles* as *experts* in an imaginary *enterprise* (this might be a full-blown "company" or simply a "responsible team"). The company or team is set up in such a way that the issue being explored is *framed* from a certain point of view. Within this *fictional context*, the children work together to carry out an important job, or *commission*, for a high-status (fictional) *client*. Along the way, they encounter problems, or *tensions* (either naturally arising, or planned and introduced by the teacher). The element of tension is essential to all drama, and in a Mantle of the Expert experience tensions add complexity to the commission, keep it interesting and promote new tasks for learning. At the same time, through episodes of *drama*, students are encouraged to explore multiple perspectives on the issues at hand and to *reflect* deeply on their learning and on the process of learning itself.

In Mantle of the Expert, curriculum is encountered in the same way as in real life: not as a set of separated "subjects" or "learning areas", but as landing points within an holistic ongoing experience. Mantle of the Expert, then, is an approach to curriculum integration. Abbott prefers the term "curriculum in*corporation*", because it resists seeing curriculum as separated in the first place (L. Abbott, personal communication, 2009). Learning in Mantle of the Expert has a strong element of inquiry, in that students may pursue their own directions and interests within the bounds of the wider commission. The possibilities for cross-curricula learning mean that the Mantle of the Expert approach is particularly well suited to the primary generalist classroom. Having said this, some secondary specialists also use the approach within particular curriculum areas, achieving focus by narrowing the commission and limiting the scope for student-led inquiry.

It can be seen from the other chapters how the core attributes of Mantle of the Expert were manifested in the examples in the research project. Teachers selected various enterprises, ranging from designers of interactive museum displays (see Chapter Five), to expert documentary researchers (see Chapter Four) and archaeologists (see Chapter Seven). The expert roles were framed as having a particular specialism or world view: the archaeologists were particularly experienced with Māori taonga (treasures), while the visitor centre designers (see Chapter Six) had a focus on sustainable practices. The commission and client in each case were chosen as suiting the children's interests and to promote curriculum tasks within the areas the teacher wished to focus on. For example, the documentary makers in Lynette's class were asked to imagine they had been commissioned by the WWF (the World Wide Fund for Nature) to carry out research and produce storyboards for a complex environmental issue (as a means to explore ethical issues and promote work in visual arts), while the cave experts in Whakarongo and Michelle's classes were commissioned by the land owners to explore and excavate the caves in a respectful way (leading to opportunities to explore ideas of respect and cultural ownership).

In every case, the curriculum tasks were framed as professional tasks that were necessary for the company to undertake. For example, instead of producing some persuasive writing as part of a "lesson" called "literacy", students in Lynette's room were asked to take a position, in writing, as part of writing a professional report for sharing at a company meeting. In Mantle of the Expert, the purpose of learning is clear and immediate. This is not learning for its own sake, nor for the teacher or "for your own good". Neither is it learning for some time in the future or for a test. Rather, it is learning because someone actually needs it done now, and needs it done well. In other words, each task is purposeful and occurs within a real-life context.

In each example from our project we can also see how drama for learning was used to explore multiple perspectives. Michelle asked children to create vignettes exploring the ethical issues arising from amateur treasure collecting. Coryn used teacher-in-role and story drama to explore a dilemma with children in role as members of a Stone Age community. Meanwhile, Whakarongo's town meeting allowed children in role to debate the pros and cons of goldmining in their town. All the teachers introduced tensions to keep students engaged. These ranged from the pressure of limited time to open a museum (Coryn's class), to the question of how to put right an accidental, but serious, breakage of a treasured object (Elicia's room), through to the chance discoveries of covert activity and threats to personal integrity (in Lynette's room). It can be seen, too, how, in every case, the teachers used a combination of teacher-led tasks and student inquiry to pursue learning goals, and that curriculum learning was approached in an incorporated way rather than within discrete boxes of time labelled as "maths" or "science" lessons.

Having identified the core elements that make up a Mantle of the Expert experience, the next and more important question to consider is *how* these components combine to influence learning. I have attempted to show this in the following table. The core elements are listed down the left side. The central column gives a definition, and in the right column an analysis is offered of how each element supports teaching and learning. The table is offered as a starting point and is expanded on, using examples from the project, over the rest of the chapter. It is worth noting that Heathcote herself identified six core elements for Mantle of the Expert practice (Heathcote & Bolton, 1994), but for our purposes I have subdivided some of these, giving a list of 10 core elements.

Table 3.1 *Ten core elements of Mantle of the Expert*

Core element	Definition	What it means for the learning
Fictional context	The children and their teacher agree to operate together in a fictional context, using their imaginations to "agree to see" or "pretend" together.	A fictional context means: • learning tasks are both playful and serious • there is dual awareness of both fictional and real worlds (*metaxis*) • safety is ensured—there are no real-world consequences • learning is not bound by real-world limitations (time, power, finance, age).
"Company", "enterprise", "responsible team"	The children and their teacher take on a collective identity as members of a collaborative enterprise or company. Sometimes this may not be a fully realised "company" but some other "responsible team" with a common goal.	Taking on a collective identity means: • learning in collaboration • a shared sense of mission, values and morals (e.g., through a mission statement) • a shared *past* history of excellence • opportunities for kinaesthetic response (e.g., setting up office space) • a real-world context
Frame	The enterprise or company is "framed" as having a particular specialism or point of view on the issues being considered. Any further roles adopted during the drama are also "framed".	• being framed as a certain "kind" of company enhances collaboration and builds shared perspectives • by framing roles, the teacher can increase or decrease the intensity of the experience and explore from a particular perspective (frame distance).
Commission	The enterprise or company is asked to undertake a particular important job.	The commission provides: • clearly expressed long-term learning goals—a shared purpose • an authentic bounded inquiry.
Client	The commission, or important job, is for a very important (fictional) client.	Involving a client means: • there is a clear purpose to the learning beyond "for the teacher" or "for its own sake" • a real-world context, that is relevant but safe • high status, high stakes, high standards • having a sense of audience, which gives a sense of obligation.
Curriculum framed as professional tasks	The tasks the children carry out in response to the commission are both appropriate curriculum tasks *and* professional tasks for the company.	Framing the curriculum as professional tasks: • provides a real-world context • gives an immediate purpose for learning • involves an "incorporated" curriculum rather than discrete "subjects".

Core element	Definition	What it means for the learning
Powerful repositioning	Children predominantly interact as "themselves" within the company, but they are positioned as *experts*: people who have been doing this a long time. The teacher positions children as knowledgeable and competent colleagues.	Power repositioning: • provides a shared sense of past success, which increases group and individual self-efficacy • involves high-status positioning—learners as experts • results in shifts in language register • causes lasting shifts in the power relationships between teacher and student.
Drama for learning/ conventions	Along with their ongoing roles within the company, children and their teacher explore the perspectives of "others"—people with alternative points of view on the issues being explored. Various "conventions of dramatic action" are used by the teacher to evoke these other roles. Heathcote listed 33 conventions, and others can also be used (see http://www. mantleoftheexpert.com).	Using drama for learning means: • multiple perspectives are explored • an embracing of complexity/ postmodernity • contesting binary/black-and-white thinking • exploring paradox and ambiguity • taking an approach that is not necessarily linear • not necessarily employing "naturalistic" drama.
Tensions	The teacher plans for certain obstacles or difficulties to arise during the completion of the commission. Often drama is used to reveal these tensions.	Introducing tensions means: • embracing the complexity and "messiness" of learning • providing authentic contexts for learning • engaging the children—maintaining their interest and intrigue • grappling and struggling, which teaches resilience.
Reflection	The teacher will allow times (both within role and out of role) for discussion and reflection on the learning *and* the learning process in multiple worlds.	Reflection involves: • meta-learning • an awareness of multiple worlds (classroom, company, client, content), which makes meta-awareness more vivid.

Core element 1: The fiction

Crucial to the operation of Mantle of the Expert is the fact that the children and teachers are operating in a fictional context. They do not form a company or responsible team in the real world, but operate in role, or at least in a shadow role (in that participants remain largely themselves but agree to act as if they were operating in the imagined context). The intention is not for students to get swept away in the imagined world, but rather to inhabit a state of *metaxis*, with an ongoing awareness of *both* the fictional world of the company and the ongoing social reality of their classroom (Boal, 1995; Edmiston, 2003).

During our project we saw evidence of children operating in a metaxical space, in which they remained aware of their ongoing identity as school children while responding as a member of the company. For example, in an interaction between classroom teacher Elicia and a child in her class, the child showed that he still saw her as "teacher" even as he was exploring his adult role: "Can you write how you spell 'established'? I want to say 'I helped established [*sic*] the company. I've been here 20 years'." As in this example, the fictional context allows the teacher and students to operate in a dual reality, where learning can be playful and serious, risky and safe, pretend and realistic. There are no real-world consequences for the actions students take, but there are plenty of real-world learnings.

Core element 2: The enterprise, company and responsible team

For some, the language of the "company" or "enterprise" might evoke somewhat unwelcome associations with business and moneymaking. However, this is not how the concept operates in Mantle of the Expert. Here the notion is closer to the one explored by Czikszentmihalyi (2003) in his explorations of collaboration or "flow" in various settings where humans collaborate, including in business. The agreement to operate as a responsible team, company or enterprise allows participants in a Mantle of the Expert experience to enter a collaborative learning arrangement with a shared sense of purpose, a set of values (often written up as a "mission statement") and, crucially, a shared past in which each person imagines "We have done this kind of thing before". It is the sense of individual and group efficacy that arises from membership of the team that is of key importance here.

Within our project, teachers reported that working in a responsible team in this way seemed to facilitate the inclusion of peers. Children previously treated as outsiders seemed to be regarded by their peers as valued members of the company. In Lynette's words:

> There seems to be a want to listen, and take on everyone's ideas. More able children lead the others, delegate and empower others to share their ideas. There's definitely more input from the children who are often disengaged.

Not every Mantle of the Expert experience involves adopting the identity of a full-blown company. Sometimes, particularly with younger children, a sense of being in a team is enough. However, the setting up of the company offices through things like defining the space, designing logos and organising communication systems is an opportunity for rich curriculum learning in itself, much of it kinaesthetic and tangible. Moreover, a full company identity can afford opportunities for teachers and students to adopt conventions of behaviour and speech that allow things to be organised and run in a formal, grown-up way (meetings, memos, pigeonholes and so on). Some teachers in our project found that they needed to remind children of the behaviour expected at board meetings, while for others, the shifts in behaviour seemed to happen as an automatic response to the repositioning. Teachers observed changes in body language, with students sitting "like adults", involving greater alertness, listening and turn-taking, along with more students opting to take notes during discussions.

Core element 3: Framing

The concept of framing, though complex, is crucial to Mantle of the Expert. Heathcote developed the concept after reading the sociological writings of Erving Goffman, who used the idea of "frame" to refer to the range of available viewpoints, or sense-making "frames", that humans inevitably bring to any social situation (Goffman, 1986). Heathcote recognised that by putting students into role, the teacher is also asking them to adopt a point of view, or "frame of reference", and suggested that a skilled teacher could plan to take this into account.

We can see how this was done in our project. For example, Lynette's students were not simply "documentary makers" but were framed as researchers with a particular dedication to telling the truth and dealing with difficult issues. This frame was established through clues, including letters from past clients and award citations. Having framed the students' role in this way early on, the teachers were later able to plan tensions that put this identity to the test. Another way teachers can manipulate the frame is to plan ways that increase or decrease the intensity of students' emotional relationship to the material. For example, in Coryn's classroom, students dealt with the world of the Stone Age through very different frames and with very different emotional involvement. As museum curators, they were distanced from the material in time and relationship. In contrast, during the episode where they took on roles as members of the community offering advice to the trainee shaman, students were taken right into the action, which increased the intensity of their personal emotional investment in the material. Such varied uses of the frame provide multiple learning opportunities within the same study.

Core element 4: The commission

The fourth core element of Mantle of the Expert is the presence of a specific commission that the enterprise, or team, is asked to undertake. The commission is generally delivered to the team a short while into the Mantle of the Expert unit, after the teacher has spent some time first building belief in the fictional enterprise. In all the examples in our research project the commission was delivered in the form of a letter. The advantage of this format for teachers and students is that the commission letter can clearly express the learning goals and set parameters for the experience. Unlike open-ended inquiry, where the teacher will support the student to go in his or her own direction, the teacher in Mantle of the Expert has a document that sets out shared goals and clear limits for the unit.

Although the students are aware that the commission is a planning device produced by the teacher, there is nonetheless a sense of being accountable to (and limited by) an "external" request. The commission has a contractual element, in that students will respond formally to it and will refer back to it for requirements. Many important learning opportunities arise from negotiating the commission. For example, in the case of Lynette's classroom, the students became concerned that they would not be able to fulfil the original specifications of the commission, so they requested a renegotiation of terms. This required formal letter writing and taking responsibility for time frames and standards.

Core element 5: The client

Associated with the commission, another important aspect of the Mantle of the Expert approach is the sense of working for an important (but fictional) client. The client is generally portrayed as someone of high status who expects top standards. For example, in Elicia's classroom, the client was a local preservation society, while in Whakarongo's class the commission came from a family of land owners. Evoking these external figures gives a clear purpose to the learning beyond doing what the teacher says or picking up skills that may be useful one day. The presence of the client gives us a clear sense of who we are working for (and "we" in this case includes the teacher). The teacher can also use role conventions to bring the client in to the classroom to check in on progress, or to attend a presentation at the end of the project. The client, then, supplies the sense of an audience to enhance the intrinsic motivation for learning that other elements can produce.

Core element 6: Curriculum tasks framed as professional tasks

Having established the enterprise, and having received a commission from a client, a range of tasks will naturally suggest themselves. In the case of the Years 5/6 museum curators in Coryn's class, for example, once the commission for the interactive museum exhibit had been received, there were endless curriculum possibilities: responding in writing to the commission; carrying out research into an aspect of Stone Age life; designing and testing interactive features of the exhibit; constructing signage; advertising; budgeting; catering for visitors; and so on. In our project, teachers found this aspect of curriculum planning a relief: instead of having to try to find ways to bring real-world contexts into their teaching, they now had a real-world context out of which curriculum tasks seemed to fall quite naturally. As Heathcote put it, "The teacher can trust any Mantle to take them to curriculum" (Heathcote, n.d. b). The challenge is to ensure the learning experiences arising are appropriate to the curriculum level and have the same integrity as traditional stand-alone tasks. As one teacher put it, "they still need to do the maths and the literacy". This is where careful teacher planning is needed.

In our project, teachers found it helpful to mix periods of student-led inquiry with teacher-led tasks. Ideally, in Mantle of the Expert, even during the teacher-led tasks teachers will avoid telling the students things, but instead look to support students to discover understandings for themselves. At the same time, Heathcote herself acknowledged that, from time to time, straight teaching has its place in Mantle of the Expert (Heathcote, n.d a). A useful strategy developed by some teachers in our project was to frame traditional teaching episodes as professional development for the company. In several cases, this was provided by a real-world expert such as a professional artist or designer coming in to the company to offer professional development.

Perhaps the most important aspect of planning tasks for Mantle of the Expert is that everything the students are asked to do should have relevance to their identity as professionals. Nothing is asked of the students unless it serves the purpose for which they are working. This is where Mantle of the Expert differs from many typical lessons, where students might be asked to carry out a piece of writing "because we are learning about persuasive writing". Here, instead, the persuasive writing has a purpose within the fictional context. For example, in Whakarongo's room, students constructed arguments for and against a proposed goldmine development, while in Lynette's room children wrote at length in an attempt to balance the two contrasting sides of the Kaimanawa horse debate.

Sequencing of tasks within Mantle of the Expert is a balance of teacher-directed planning and emergent inquiry. Sometimes the teacher will take the learning in a particular direction to fulfil a preplanned intention or to lead into a particular task they want the children to undertake. At other times the teacher might respond to quite unexpected directions emerging from the work. For teachers who like to be thoroughly planned in advance, the more flexible aspects can be a challenge. One of the teachers in the project, Lynette, admits that she struggled with emergent inquiry at first, but ultimately found it empowering:

> For teachers starting out the scary thing is you feel you are not owning it—you don't know where you are going next. Every day after school I'd be thinking 'Where are we going next?' But it's actually great … Or to put it another way, you are owning it *more*—you are right inside it. You become more caught up in it. I think that's the beauty of it.

The important challenge for teachers, of course, is to ensure the children themselves understand the direction of the experience and are not confused by shifts in direction. Elicia found that "storying" the emergent adventure on the classroom walls was a very useful device, while other teachers made use of class blogs for a similar purpose. One challenge experienced by several teachers in our project was how to work with children who had missed out on part of the Mantle of the Expert experience. This seemed particularly difficult where children missed early stages of the programme and had not been part of the co-construction of the company identity.

Core element 7: Conscious repositioning of students

Issues of power and positioning are absolutely pivotal to Mantle of the Expert. The way children are invited to take on roles, and the ways these roles are framed, leads to a conscious repositioning of relationships and an attempt to shift the way power operates within the classroom. First of all the children are repositioned as members of the team or company. It is important to note that while in role in the company, students are not expected to take on a character any different from their own. Though some teachers in our project favoured the use of name tags with made-up names, this is not necessary: children are essentially playing themselves but adopting the position of experienced professionals in a particular field. The most important aspect of the company or team role is the way the students are positioned—by the teacher and the other students— as both competent and experienced. The aim of this repositioning is to prime the students' and the teacher's attitude so that they encounter new learnings and new knowledge from a place of self-efficacy. Learning is presented as a growing-on of existing expertise rather than as a leap into unknown territory. This is one of the most subtle, and yet most fundamental, cornerstones of Mantle of the Expert teaching.

Teachers involved in our research noticed a difference in student self-efficacy, which they attributed to this repositioning of students. As Lynette put it, "The drama put them 'up there', and they wanted to remain." Teachers also reported that this sense of self-efficacy seemed to persist beyond the intervention. Several weeks after the end of the Mantle of the Expert experience, teachers felt that children were still interacting with each other, and the teacher, from this position of competence. Children, too, noted the lasting shift in relationship that occurred through working in Mantle of the Expert, as in this quote from a child in Lynette's class:

> MOTE [Mantle of the Expert] gave Room 10 a chance to be 'adults' ... It was really interesting to discuss and be with people in the class when they are being 'adults' because it was very different than when we are doing work normally. Because everyone is treated equally it is amazing when children and teachers alike all come together to work.

Though more research is needed into the effects of repositioning on student achievement in the context of Mantle of the Expert, other studies have been carried out in which repositioning of subjects has been found to significantly improve achievement (e.g., Kahnemann, 2012).

The repositioning of students in a Mantle of the Expert classroom is made manifest in a number of ways. For example, Elicia experimented with alternatives to the classroom tradition of putting up your hand. Several of the teachers reorganised the space to reflect the equality of teachers and students during meetings (sitting on chairs rather than the floor, rotating the position of "chair" for the meetings, using pigeonholes or memos to share important information). Perhaps the most obvious way of signalling a shift in agency is through the teacher's talk, and indeed our researchers saw teachers shifting to a quite different register when speaking to the students in role as experts.

More important than any of these outward indicators of power shifting is the underlying shift in attitude that is required, as Elicia describes here:

> It's really easy when teaching to think you've handed the power over but that can be a trap. There's a difference between saying 'Here you have my permission to take some power now' and the kids understanding the power they already have within them. The kind of thing I'm talking about here is something I've only noticed within a mantle. It's not a sudden shift or a gift from the teacher. It's a subtle process of growing into status. It is evidenced in their body language and their side conversations with you and with each other.

This fundamental shift in attitude is not always an easy move for teachers to make because it does imply a ceding of agency in a situation where some teachers are very concerned with managing and controlling the class.

Another reason why the repositioning of students may be challenging for some teachers is that it has quasi-political overtones, to do with shifting the underlying locus of power within the classroom, the school and even the wider world. Brian Edmiston expresses this very well:

> One of the core reasons why as a teacher I use drama is because when we create an imagined world, we can imagine that we frame events differently so that our power and authority relationships are changed. A long-term aim of mine as a teacher is as much as possible to share power and authority with students. I want students to have more opportunities to use words and deeds to act appropriately but in ways that are often not sanctioned in classrooms.

> Additionally I hope that students' sense of their personal and shared authority will become more secure and more extended while at the same time more aware of others' authority. I want a culture to develop that is more egalitarian than most students expect walking into the room. (Edmiston, 2003, p. 225)

As Edmiston's words imply, the reconceptualising of children that occurs within Mantle of the Expert is, for many teachers, part of a deliberate attempt to reconceptualise young people within the real world. For many teachers, using Mantle of the Expert is not using an approach so much as adopting a world view.

Core element 8: Drama for learning

Along with the roles set up within the company or team, the teacher using Mantle of the Expert will plan additional role-based activities so that children have the chance to explore different points of view on the issues being explored. For example, in Michelle's classroom the students (in company role as cave experts) were invited to step into the past and role-play a moment in the lives of the earliest dwellers in the cave. An important artefact from this episode (an arrowhead, lovingly carved) was then shown, in another episode, being handled disrespectfully by a modern-day visitor. In Lynette's room children had the opportunity to take on roles as protesters, police officers and even horses as they explored the different perspectives on the issue of the Kaimanawa horses.

Dramatic role-taking permits the exploration of multiple viewpoints by giving students the opportunity to "walk in the shoes" of people other than themselves. It even moves them beyond their responses as experts within the company. The adopting of multiple perspectives strengthens the children's reflective discussion and supports them to realise that there are multiple possible answers to any given issue.

Heathcote has identified 33 different drama conventions that can be utilised to deepen role-taking, so that students can not only walk in the shoes of someone else but might also speak their thoughts, write their words, ask or respond to questions, engage in dialogue with another and so on (see role conventions at http://www.mantleoftheexpert.com). In our project, the teachers were more familiar with the process drama conventions as identified in *The New Zealand Curriculum* (for example, freeze frame, hotseating, spoken thoughts) and so tended to make use of these (Ministry of Education, 2000, pp. 48–49).

It is not only the children who can take multiple roles within a drama-for-learning segment of a Mantle of the Expert experience. The teacher can also take on different identities through teaching in role. The teacher can choose from a variety of different status positions and so utilise their role-taking for a number of different purposes (Edmiston, 2003). Within our project, teachers adopted roles in order to bring information to the team, represent a point of view, issue a challenge or introduce a new problem. For example, Coryn took on the role of village elder during a drama-for-learning episode in her class. She evoked an atmosphere of respect and seriousness while the children in role as people of the village discussed whether a young woman from the village should become a shaman or stay with her family. Elicia took on the role of Joseph Banks, the botanist who travelled with James Cook, to describe to the archaeology team the way New Zealand looked and sounded when he first arrived, and to ask for their help in reproducing the lost pages of his sketchbook. Some teachers in this project were more comfortable relying on more experienced teachers to take on the roles in their classrooms and invited outside teachers in as in-role visitors. It may be worth mentioning, too, that in this project the researchers also took on roles at times, including one researcher going into role as an apprentice to hold learning conversations with the children as they 'showed her the ropes' in the company.

There is insufficient space here to describe the many benefits for learning that arise from role-taking. However, one of the key benefits is the capacity to explore multiple perspectives and the breaking down of binary black-and-white thinking. In drama we are not bound by one identity (we can walk in different shoes and see the issue through other people's eyes). Nor are we bound by time (we can see the same moment over and over, change it or play out several possibilities at once). We are not bound by conventions of social behaviour (we can shift the conventions to play a moment naturalistically, melodramatically or in a range of different ways). Nor are we bound by rules of nature or physics (we can hear people's thoughts, see through walls or invoke a magic potion to force someone to speak the truth). Far from being "just" pretend, drama is an emancipatory device that frees its participants from the constraints of reality. Drama encourages an embracing of complexity by acknowledging and embodying multiple "truths". This was illustrated within our project when one of the children in Lynette's class, grappling with how to portray both sides of the Kaimanawa horse issue, stated, "I don't think there *is* such a thing as one truth." One wonders whether he could have reached such a conclusion without having engaged with all the different stakeholders through drama. In the broadest sense, then, drama offers children access to a post-structuralist view of reality, with its inherent openness to multiple perspectives. As O'Neill has pointed out, process drama's postmodern, fragmented, nonlinear way of presenting the world also aligns it with developments in contemporary theatre performers (O'Neill, 1995, p. xvii).

Core element 9: Tensions

Whether in the theatre, television or children's socio-dramatic play, all effective drama relies on tension. The same is true in classroom drama, where, as Heathcote puts it, "the teacher puts the tension in and the rest follows" (quoted in Smedley, 1971). Throughout a Mantle of the Expert experience, then, the teacher will plan for certain obstacles or difficulties to arise. To help in planning for these tensions, Heathcote offers a taxonomy of 12 levels of tensions, which outlines the different qualities, or intensity, of each tension.[1] At level 1 of the scale, the teacher might evoke

---

1   See http://www.mantleoftheexpert.com

a vague sense of tension by implying someone is watching or scrutinising the company. A slightly more intense tension can be conjured up through pressure of time (level 7 on the scale). At the very top of the list comes "loss of faith in some companions". Here the teacher might plan an episode in which someone in the company (a fictional "other", of course, not one of the actual children) has carried out their work inadequately. As well as ongoing "productive" tensions, the teacher may plan to introduce a particularly challenging "key tension" that really tests the mettle of the company. For example, in the case of the documentary makers in Lynette's class, a serious case of subterfuge was uncovered and the members of the company were placed in an ethical dilemma about whether they should report it and thereby betray a friend.

Using tensions like this serves a number of purposes. First of all, tensions or problems are a part of life, so by introducing them the teacher can offer authentic contexts for learning in which learning is complex and messy and not overly simplified. Second, tensions help maintain a sense of interest and intrigue in the drama. Children become accustomed to the fact that twists and turns are to be expected, and this builds their engagement in learning and makes it fun. Third, and significantly, tensions mean that children have to "grapple" in order to learn. They are not simply given expert status in an empty way, but are encouraged to earn and justify that position. The skills, understanding and attitudes that have been so carefully set up in the early stages of the drama (through the timeline, mission statement, profiles, etc.) are tested through the tensions, challenging the child to defend their point of view and operate from that heightened state of agency. The mantle of expertise is not given, but earned and worked for in a gradual and authentic way.

Core element 10: Reflection

A final, but crucial, element of Mantle of the Expert is reflection. The teacher will allow times (both inside and outside the fictional frame) for participants to engage in discussion and reflection on the learning that is taking place. The dual realities operating within the Mantle of the Expert classroom make the learning context very explicit and a distanced relationship, which enhances reflection on what is being learned. As Edmiston (2003) points out, the participant in Mantle of the Expert is always aware of *both* the "as if" *and* the "as is" worlds operating together. The teacher can, at any time, signal a step out of the fictional company back into the real-life classroom to discuss and evaluate what is being learned "over there" in the fictional context. In our project we found that one of the simplest yet most effective reflection strategies was for a teacher who had been working in role with the children to step out of role and ask, "So what happened while I was away?" Children were happy to recap and reflect on the work they had just done, even when they were aware this was the very same teacher they had just been working with in role. At other times, children asked teachers to move into role so that they could explain something that the teacher in role figure needed to understand.

The dual realities of Mantle of the Expert encourage reflection not only on *what* is being learned but *how* it is being learned. As *The New Zealand Curriculum* (Ministry of Education, 2007) reminds us, the ability to notice the ways one is learning (meta-learning) is an important skill and one that should be fostered by teachers. Mantle of the Expert, with its clearly signalled multiple contexts, brings the child's awareness of their learning into consciousness and makes the structures under which learning is happening very explicit. With skilful questioning and negotiation the teacher can encourage students to reflect on how the learning is going, and even renegotiate aspects of the learning environment before stepping back into it. All teachers who used Mantle of the Expert in our project remarked on this as a key feature of their experience with the children.

Indeed, in our project we found evidence of children continuing to reflect on the systems and structures of their learning even beyond the Mantle of the Expert intervention. For example, in one classroom, some weeks after the Mantle of the Expert experience was over, some students respectfully asked the teacher whether they might re-organise the reading groups. In our view, it is exciting to think that Mantle of the Expert might encourage this kind of agentic positioning of learners.

Conclusion

This chapter has attempted to outline 10 core components of Mantle of the Expert. Of course none of these components works in isolation: each depends on the others to be successful. For example, it is not enough to simply tell students they are experts: if a genuine shift in *power and positioning* is to occur, the teacher must spend time building belief in the *company*. Similarly, if the teacher wishes to introduce *tensions* to really challenge the students, they will need to plan tensions that confront the values and shared history set up within the *company identity*. The subtle and sophisticated teaching required to interweave the components of Mantle of the Expert has led to its being described as a "system", which takes years to learn to use successfully (Abbott, 2007, p. 3). Though complex, the "system" provides structures and practices that seem— almost in and of themselves—to encourage shifts within the traditional classroom attitudes to teaching, learning and the curriculum.

The complexity of Mantle of the Expert should not be viewed as a discouragement to teachers interested in trying the approach. The teacher's learning in how to use Mantle of the Expert can be seen in the same light as learning for the children in the fictional enterprise. With time and experience, and a striving for high standards, the "mantle" of experience and expertise will surely grow around the teacher's shoulders. In the case of our project, all the teachers were relatively inexperienced in Mantle of the Expert and, apart from attendance at a 3-day conference, had had very little exposure to it. Nevertheless, with the support of members of the research team and each other, these teachers were able to introduce features of the approach into their classrooms and see the effects. The teachers involved would all say that they learned from the experience and all have seen it as worthwhile to continue to develop their practice. Like any complex teaching approach, the teacher wishing to use Mantle of the Expert must be willing to embark on an ongoing learning experience akin to an apprenticeship. However, it is an apprenticeship that can be started at any time and, in the case of teachers in this project, one that is gladly continued.

References

Abbott, L. (2007). *Mantle of the Expert 2: Training materials and tools.* Essex, UK: Essex County Council.

Boal, A. (1995). *The rainbow of desire: The Boal method of theatre and therapy.* New York, NY: Routledge.

Bolton, G. (2003). *Dorothy Heathcote's story: Biography of a remarkable drama teacher.* Stoke on Trent, UK: Trentham Books.

Carroll, J., Anderson, M., & Cameron, D. (2006). *Real players?: Drama, technology and education.* Stoke on Trent, UK: Trentham Books.

Czikszentmihalyi, H. (2003). *Good business: Leadership, flow and the making of meaning.* New York: Penguin.

Edmiston, B. (2003). What's my position?: Role, frame and positioning when using process drama. *Research in Drama Education: The Journal of Applied Theatre and Performance, 8*(2), 221–229.

Erikkson, S. A. (2011). Distancing at close range: Making strange devices in Dorothy Heathcote's process drama: Teaching political awareness through drama. *Research in Drama Education: The Journal of Applied Theatre and Performance, 16*(1), 101–123.

Goffman, E. (1986). *Frame analysis: An essay on the organisation of experience.* Boston, MA: Northeastern University Press.

Heathcote, D. (2009). *Mantle of the Expert: My current understanding.* Keynote address to the Weaving Our Stories: International Mantle of the Expert conference, University of Waikato, Hamilton.

Heathcote, D. (n.d. a). *Drama for living: A twentyfirst century vision for education* [video recording]. Address given at Trinity College, Dublin.

Heathcote, D. (n.d. b). *Education through drama: Planning with Heathcote* [video recording]. New York: Insight Media.

Heathcote, D., & Bolton, G. (1994). *Drama for learning: Dorothy Heathcote's Mantle of the Expert approach to education.* Portsmouth, NH: Heinemann Press.

Heston, S. (1993). *The Dorothy Heathcote archive.* Manchester: Manchester Metropolitan University. Retrieved from http://www.did.stu.mmu.ac.uk/dha/hcheston.asp

Kahnemann, D. (2012). *Thinking fast and slow.* London: Penguin Books.

Ministry of Education. (2007). *The New Zealand curriculum.* Wellington: Learning Media.

Ministry of Education. (2000). *Arts in the New Zealand curriculum.* Wellington: Learning Media.

O'Neill, C. (1995). *Drama worlds: A framework for process drama.* Portsmouth, NH: Heinemann Press.

Smedley, R. (1971). *Three looms waiting.* BBC Omnibus documentary. Retrieved from http://www.youtube.com/watch?v=f5jBNIEQrZs

Further resources

Mantle of the Expert (NZ) website: http://www.mantleoftheexpert.co.nz
Mantle of the Expert (UK) website: http://www.mantleoftheexpert.com

CHAPTER FOUR

Searching for the Truth/s:
Exploring Enviro-ethics

Viv Aitken with Lynette Townsend

Introduction

Fig 4.1 *Lynette's class in role as* PSP *receiving their imaginary TVNZ awards*

This unit of work took place in a Years 5/6 class in a high-decile urban primary school. Children in the class came from a mix of ethnicities. The majority of children were of European and Asian extraction, with four Māori, one Pasifika and one child from Africa.

Initial planning was undertaken as a joint project between the classroom teacher, Lynette Townsend; deputy principal, Gay Gilbert; and Viv Aitken, from the Faculty of Education at the University of Waikato. This unit of work was also taught as part of a teacher education programme, so a group of Viv's student teachers were involved in some of the teaching. Although this particular version of the unit involved several teachers' input it should be stressed that it could have been taught by just one teacher, and indeed Lynette had sole charge of the class for most of the 7 weeks.

In this Mantle of the Expert unit children were in role as preproduction researchers for a documentary production company with a particular reputation for fairness. The company was commissioned to carry out research for a documentary telling the stories behind the management of Kaimanawa horses (feral horses found in the Kaimanawa ranges in New Zealand, whose numbers are controlled by annual culling). The fictional client chosen for the drama was the World Wide Fund for Nature (WWF), who asked the company to produce three storyboards of possible angles on this issue.

Planning for the unit took some time. The starting point for planning was a photo in the local newspaper showing some Kaimanawa horses at the annual muster. As Lynette recalls, the photo was very evocative:

> It was so expressive. The aggressive way the horses were rearing up. They looked in a bad condition and the image conveyed the whole issue of being penned in. We knew that straight away the children would go "poor horses" and we wanted to eventually give the other side too.

Figure 4.2 *Kaimanawa horse muster (original image from* Waikato Times, *2010; reprinted with permission)*

One of the reasons for choosing this context was that the children had so much compassion towards animals. It is well known that children at this age are drawn to studies of animals, so this context was age appropriate. At the time, also, Lynette had just finished a different Mantle of the

Expert unit with an animal theme and felt it would be useful to deepen the children's understanding.

The big idea

The big idea underlying this unit of work was decided from the outset. Lynette wanted to explore an ethical dilemma in animal rights. By working in role as expert researchers, children were encouraged to explore different and contrasting perspectives on the Kaimanawa horse issue. Through a gradual process of unfolding tensions and interactions with fictional characters, the children were exposed to two contradictory views. On one side was a (fictional) protest group, Wild and Free, who were opposed to the culling of horses, and on the other was the Department of Conservation (DOC), who wished to protect the native flora and fauna threatened by the horses.

In choosing to make the company researchers for a documentary company rather than making them responsible for the whole documentary, the teachers deliberately narrowed the focus to emphasise the ethical aspects rather than the technicalities of documentary making. Of course, a Mantle of the Expert experience about the technical aspects of documentary making would have been valid, and educational, but it was not the chosen direction this time. As Lynette remarked, "We didn't want this unit to try and cover everything about documentary making otherwise it would have been huge and would have distracted from the key learning." The choice of company, and frame, was made to help focus the learning in the desired direction: in this case, the issue of ethics and multiple perspectives.

For a teacher planning for Mantle of the Expert it can be tempting to throw the net wide and encourage a wide-ranging company identity, especially when the various possibilities for inquiry are so rich and exciting. It is true, too, as Dorothy Heathcote remarks, that "any company will lead to curriculum" (*Education through drama*, n.d.). However, by carefully planning for a company with a narrow specialism, the teacher can support children to work in a more focused way towards a particular locus of learning, with the result that learning becomes deep rather than broad.

Having established the company, the commission and a series of tensions that might arise in the fulfilling of the commission, the teachers were ready to begin the Mantle of the Expert adventure.

The hook

The unit itself started with a dramatic convention. Children were asked to look at a live effigy or statue (sometimes called a freeze frame) in which a student teacher had taken the role of an elderly woman protester holding a sign. Initially the sign was blank. Then, after urging from the children, words were added. Lynette remembers: "It was clever the way we didn't have words on the sign at first. Children had to brainstorm and interpret *'What have we got here?'*"

Fig 4.3 *The 'hook': student teachers in role*

The tension was built by having additional details added to the effigy one by one. The children were encouraged to interpret and reinterpret what they were seeing, until finally there was a complete tableau showing the protester, a police officer arresting her and a horse being euthanised by a vet.

This gradual revealing of the scene was designed to capture interest and pique curiosity. Many teachers will be familiar with similar elicitation and disclosure strategies used with photographs in social studies lessons (Ministry of Education, 1997). This practice of deliberately holding back information and enticing the group to "earn" understanding through cognitive grappling is one of the key features of the Mantle of the Expert approach (Heston, n.d.).

Next, the children were invited to interview Penelope the protester and get her perspective. Viv took the role of Penelope and deliberately answered questions in a way that encouraged children to sympathise with her point of view. To signal her move into role, Viv donned the same orange scarf worn by the protestor in the effigy. This conscious use of "signing" is a key feature of Mantle of the Expert teaching. As Heathcote (1984) notes, all teachers use signs and symbols to communicate, but in Mantle of the Expert the signing process becomes both more conscious and more theatrical:

> In the theatre all actors sign for the benefit of the audience. In life we signal for the other person out of need for response. In teaching we make our signs specially interpretable, so that the children are able to read all signals with the least possible confusion. We deliberately sign for the responder to come into active participation in the event. (p. 161)

The scarf became a potent symbol throughout the 7 weeks of the Mantle experience. As later photos in this chapter show, different members of the class, including children, adopted the scarf when they wanted to take the role of Penelope and speak from her perspective. The placard, too, was returned to time and again as a symbol for the protesters' perspective.

Fig 4.4 The placard and headscarf

After the children had spoken to Penelope and gained sympathy for her, the attention shifted towards forming the company. An inquiry question was asked: "Who is there who would tell this woman's story?" and a discussion ensued about the kinds of professional companies there might be in the world to tell stories like this. Through this kind of questioning, the teachers led the children towards the idea of being documentary makers.

Organising for learning

Having established that they would be taking on the role of documentary researchers, Lynette and the class spent substantial time building belief in the company identity. Lynette describes how this began with the co-

construction of the office door—another important symbol: "The door was like a portal to our company. They spent quite a lot of time on that—choosing plants and images to give the right impression to the customers."

Next, the floor space of the office was mapped out. Lynette used the opportunity to teach the children about drawing to scale and they practised this as a homework task before working together on the company offices. One of the children discovered a 3D modelling program online, and this

was used to create a virtual tour around the building.

Fig 4.5 *The doorway to* PSP *offices*

At this point a company noticeboard was established and teachers prepared a number of letters and communications from past clients, which were placed on the noticeboard to "remind" the company what they were renowned for. Children read and digested these communications and used the information to create a company mission statement.

COMPANY MISSION STATEMENT

Problem Solving People (PSP) is an honest company who are dedicated, have integrity and always take people, the environment and animals into account.

As a company we wish to provide you with an honest and sustainable resolution that is hopefully compatible with you.

PSP researches first, then interviews both sides of the story to find out the truth and raise public awareness.

One of our many values is saving Animals and Nature. PSP respects clients' opinions and we are always sensitive and caring. We will listen to multiple perspectives within the community.

PSP always strives to achieve high standards. We work hard to ensure that our customers feel secure and well respected.

The co-construction of a mission statement like this can be a critical part of the groundwork to a successful Mantle of the Expert. Lynette noted:

> I think it's really important how the 'givens' of the company are put into the mission statement. A number of the children kept referring back to that mssion statement and saying, 'We need to do things this way, because we are that kind of company.'

In the early stages the mission statement encouraged the children to take ownership of their company. Later it became a tool to reflect on how to conduct themselves responsibly and, as such, was referred back to time and again. As Lynette put it, "The letters from clients put them 'up there' [in a high ethical position] and then they wanted to remain there."

The children also built belief by writing CVs and designing business cards. Commitment to role was also built through drama when the company received notification from a (fictional) national television service that they had won an award for a past project. Through dramatic enactments the children imagined key events from the day of the award ceremony.

Not all children fully invested in their company role at this stage of the unit. Indeed, some seemed quite hesitant and unsure about the experience. Fortunately, the teachers knew that this was to be expected, especially with children who had not experienced Mantle of the Expert before. As Bolton (2003) reminds us:

> They are not required to be in role in the usual dramatic sense, but must tacitly accede to the taking on of the expert mantle. Depending on the social health of the class and the appeal of the fiction, this will take time and may even fluctuate in commitment from day to day. (p. 129)

Individually, children began to exhibit signs of role acceptance, such as the girl who created a paper briefcase and brought it to meetings, and the boys who worked extra hours adding details to the company doors. At about this stage in the process Lynette recalls that some children started to make use of the company noticeboard for their own communications in role as company members:

> Children added things to the noticeboard throughout. For example, someone made up a tournament for company social games, posted that on the noticeboard and we ended up actually doing some of these activities in our PE time.

Once the children felt secure in their role as researchers, they were supported to carry out self-directed research into the Kaimanawa horses issue. Lynette was struck by how motivated the children were by the sense of wider purpose. Children continued their research at home, over lunchtimes and before and after school. To assist with the sense of belief in the fictional world, homework tasks were framed as "company memos".

Lynette was careful to ensure the research was not only focused and purposeful but also led to curriculum learning of quality. She guided the study towards statistical investigations of horse numbers, culling figures and projected population numbers. The class formed their own research questions and, using real-world resources, they explored their questions and graphed the results.

The gradual process of building belief in the company's collective identity brought with it an increasing sense of responsibility and maturity. In the early stages of the unit the teachers noticed that the students were very focused on themselves as individuals. But then, as their belief in the company gradually built up through things like the business cards and CVs, it became more about a collective company identity. Lynette noted a gradual but marked shift from *I* to *we* language:

> You can see why that building belief stage is pivotal to move them to a place where they really are part of the company. I don't know how you could do it without this—it's what makes it have a collaborative feel.

Fig 4.6 *Discussion group with a student teacher*

Fig 4.7 *Self-directed research using class laptops*

Deepening the learning

The class had been working steadily for several weeks when the first of the dramatised "productive tensions" was introduced. Children had discovered through their research that, after the muster, people can buy Kaimanawa horses for domestic use. It was easy for children to leap to this as a "solution" to the problem of what to do with the horses. Teachers wanted to raise the question, "What makes a suitable home for a horse?" and thereby encourage deeper thinking.

Fig 4.8 *The vignette of Billy and his family*

Fig 4.9 *Children reproduce the scene to explore different perspectives*

APPLICATION FORM
Please complete details in full

Name..........................
Address.................
Phone number..........................

Please read and sign the following:

I understand that Kaimanawa horses are wild creatures and that the decision to adopt a horse is a serious commitment.
I will take full responsibility for meeting the horse's needs.
I will meet all costs of transporting the horse from the muster to my property.

Signed...............................

Date...............................

****

The tension was introduced by showing the class a short scene, or vignette. (In this case the vignette was enacted by a group of student-teachers. A teacher working alone could use a photograph, a preprepared video clip or even invite members of the class to create a scene in advance.) This vignette was silent, and showed a young boy's distress at having his pet Kaimanawa horse taken away to the meatworks. It was implied that this was because his family had been unable to care for the horse properly. Using dramatic conventions, the children were invited to speak the thoughts and feelings of this boy and his family and to discuss why Billy's family hadn't told him the truth about what was happening.

> I'm wishing money would grow on trees. [Child speaking the thoughts of the father]
>
> I'm sure we can find the money. [Child speaking the thoughts of the mother]
>
> Lying! Why would they need to lie? [Child speaking the thoughts of Billy]
>
> It's called a white lie—they lied to not make him feel upset, because the truth would hurt. [Child's comment during out-of-role discussion]

The children were invited to critique the process that led to the family being in this situation. They were shown an application form and asked whether this was adequate for the purpose of screening suitable owners. The children had many ideas on how to amend the application form to give the necessary information about the prospective owner, their intentions and their past history. The application forms the children came up with allowed rich learning about questioning and formal writing, and also opened up new areas for research. As one child said, "We can't possibly make a decent form unless we know more about what a horse needs to keep it alive."

A second productive tension was introduced when the company received a letter from DOC challenging the documentary team to include the scientific perspective on the horse issue. The deputy principal, Gay, visited the classroom in role as a DOC scientist and put forward the argument that the horse culls were very important to protect the flora of the area, some of which is found nowhere else in the world. Initially there was some resistance to hearing this point of view. Children became quite heated and defended the pro-horse perspective and quoted (real-world) statistics to back up their arguments. But after a while they listened to what she had to say and the teacher-in-role was able to challenge them to find out more about what DOC did if they were really going to tell the truth of this story.

It was at this point in the unit that children came to the crux of the ethical dilemma, as planned by the teachers. Suddenly they were challenged to consider the value of life itself rather than just being swept up in an emotive concern only for life in its more appealing forms.

A science-based session followed in which children worked in small groups with the student-teachers. The company was informed (by letter) that DOC workers would be happy to talk to them, but as busy scientists they could not take time out of their field work. So, the company was invited to accompany the scientists to the Kaimanawa ranges, work alongside them and discuss the horse issue with them at the same time. In actual fact the "field trip" took place to imagined sites in and around the classroom, which children were asked to "agree to see" as the wild hills of the ranges. The fictional set-up allowed student-teachers to organise hands-on science experiments appropriate to the curriculum level, which children carried out while also holding discussions on the wider issues of the horses and their impacts on the land. Lynette recalled:

> It was great to see them out there with all their equipment and their gloves etc. They did experiments on erosion, plants and the different lengths of flax roots. They did observational drawing. They looked at the different species of native plants unique to that area. It was a powerful day. The children were incredibly engaged. They learned a huge amount from that.

Fig 4.10 *Children working with student teachers in role as DOC scientists*

In this case the children worked in small groups with one student-teacher per group. It was very helpful to have multiple adults in the room. A teacher working alone could achieve something similar by setting up a number of self-directed tasks and circulating between them in role as a DOC scientist giving advice and opinions.

Now that they had established the opposing perspectives of Penelope and the anti-cull protesters on one hand, and the DOC scientists on the other, the children moved into creating their storyboards. This was a testing time as children grappled with what point of view they should suggest for the documentary. Children produced written discussions expressing the arguments for and against the issue. In the samples that follow, the children's original spelling has been preserved:

> If DOC doesn't kill the Kaimanawa horses they will eat all the native plants and there will be no Kaimanawa horses and no native plants. When DOC kills them they try to give it to new homes first. As well, they go to a pet food factory for cats and dogs. Penelope things it's rotten business killing introduced Kaimanawa horses ... I agree with DOC because the Kaimanawa horses will die of starvation after they eat all the plants.

> The department of conservation can't be trusted. They said they will leave 500 horses in the wild but there are only 300 left and they are still mustering our unique wild horses that are dying horrible deaths and getting sent to [the] pet food factory. How will you feel about that? Imagine if you were a Kaimanawa horse, being chased by a helicopter and herded into a small little space and if you don't get sold it's the pet food factory for you.

> Penelope is furious about people killing horses and has been most of her life. She has been a passionate horse lover since a little girl ... People think they shouldn't care about a measly old woman but Kaimanawas helped her get to school for an education and when she had tonsillitis she rode seven miles for the medication.

The writing task encouraged children to explore the complex notions of right and wrong that had emerged from their work and to think about how such opposing views might both be respected. Lynette was careful not to determine the direction of their thinking, but to allow children to come to their own conclusions.

The level of thinking displayed by some children at this point was very impressive. Perhaps the most memorable moment was when one child in the class stated during a company meeting, "I don't think there [is] such a thing as one truth!", displaying a level of epistemological understanding well beyond that expected of a primary school child.

Now halfway through the unit, the children needed to consolidate what they had learned and present their storyboard ideas. The original commission asked for three storyboards of six images, with captions. At this point the children decided they needed to renegotiate the commission. A letter was sent to the client asking if the number of storyboards could be reduced from three to two. This would allow the company to produce one storyboard from Penelope's point of view and one from DOC's.

With the focus on producing storyboards, Lynette called on a real-world expert, visual art lecturer Graham Price, to come and teach the class about image making and storyboarding. His visit to the class was framed as "professional development" for the company, which allowed him to conduct the session as a teacher-led skills-teaching session.

Fig 4.11 *Visit from a real world expert, framed as 'professional development'*

Lynette's knowledge in this area was limited, so she welcomed Graham's support:

> He taught them about angles, colours, a lot of terminology and specifics of visual language—how to connect with the viewer. To shift the children to the next level, we needed that level of expertise.

Bringing in outside experts from among the parents and the wider community is a valuable way to inject the required knowledge and skills that may go beyond the teacher's capacity.

The children worked fairly intensively on their storyboards for approximately 2 weeks. Drawing on what they had learned from Graham, they created a set of images using some photographs sourced from the Internet and manipulated by software and other photographs taken with their own cameras. They considered sequencing, angles, colour, size and mood as they created the storyboards. The re-editing process occurred up to four times.

 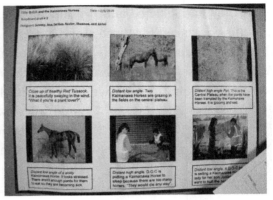

Fig 4.12 *Working hard to get the details of storyboards right*

The storyboard work was conducted as self-directed work in small groups, which was challenging for some. Lynette recalled the technical issues associated with things like booking computers, saving the files correctly and working between PCs and Macs. At the same time, she noticed that new children took leadership roles because of their technical abilities. She was very struck by how committed children were to the quality of the work they wished to produce.

Children's reflections show that they, too, were pleased with their own resilience and relationships during the storyboarding process. One student wrote, "Everyone in my group compelled each other to keep going even when we never thought we could finish the commission." Another hints at some tensions within the group that were overcome: "Our group all tolerated each other ... we had important roles that all came together in the end." Almost all comments hint at the hard work that went into this phase of the unit:

> One of the positives is we never gave up especially when our folder got deleted.

> Our team really are caring for each other. When someone is down we got them back on their feet.

For a small number of children, this phase of the Mantle was challenging in terms of having to negotiate and agree in their small groups. Lynette was impressed with how the children coped with the challenges:

> I said to them, 'Do you want to regroup?' I offered one child the chance to join another group, but he said, 'No, I'll see it through,' which was very adult like.

In these children's comments can be seen graphic examples of the real issues involved in collaboration. They represent children's authentic opportunities to practise the key competency of *relating to others* (Ministry of Education, 2007).

The final, key dramatic tension was introduced towards the end of the process. Student-teachers went into role as cadets from the army and delivered a document to the company (once again, for a teacher working alone this could have been achieved through one teacher working in teacher-in-role). The cadets brought a transcript of an intercepted conversation they had recorded in an army exercise on the Kaimanawa Ranges. In order to understand the transcript, which had no punctuation, the children had to add these features and think about how the words might have been spoken. In other words, the paper became a kind of script: a means for students to discuss grammatical features and features of the voice such as emphasis, volume and pause.

The intercepted message revealed that Penelope's protest group was planning to purchase Kaimanawa horses at the next muster and then re-release them, thereby undermining the whole DOC programme of population control. The company decided they needed to confront Penelope with this information. When they did so, Penelope asked them to play down this aspect of the story and not include it in the documentary.

Thus the ethical dilemma took on an even more complex moral dimension. Lynette remembers this as being an important moment for the students:

Fig 4.13 Grappling with the ethical issues

It was hugely powerful. Several of the students had a strong viewpoint. 'We can't just cover this up.' They went back to the mission statement and their givens. But more than this, it was about being true to themselves. This deep learning came through in some of the profound things the children said later.

The work on the storyboards was finally completed and a session was held in which the completed storyboards were formally presented to the client. The presence of the client was represented by a sheet of paper with the WWF logo on it.

Fig 4.14 *The client arrives (represented in symbolic form on paper)*

According to Lynette, the children completely accepted this representation: "I did like the way it was a symbol instead of a real person. It didn't have any less impact, in fact they treated the symbol with huge respect." For teachers learning about Mantle of the Expert, especially those teaching solo, it is important to realise that you do not always need to adopt a role in person. Symbols like this can elegantly serve to evoke a dramatic "other". Indeed, Heathcote (1984) lists 33 possible conventions available to teachers to evoke roles, each with a subtly different purpose and impact.

The children presented their storyboards, both in hard copy and through dramatic presentation. All children, including those who had been quite uncertain about adopting dramatic roles at the start of the 7-week unit, now performed with focus and seriousness. They had experienced drama as a learning tool regularly in their classes and they were deeply engaged with the material. Out of this, children now demonstrated a marked increase in confidence and skills in drama as an art form.

Fig 4.15 *Performing the storyboards to the client*

The closing ritual for the unit was a version of the dramatic convention "conscience alley", in which the class formed two lines and one by one spoke the thoughts of the client as he left the presentation. The value of this was that, instead of receiving praise or affirmation from the teachers, the ritual allowed children to reflect on their own work from the perspective of the fictional outsider. The teachers deliberately built the intensity of this moment, and children were silent and focused, even when the lunch bell rang midway through the exercise. As the ritual was completed there was quite a release of emotion. Lynette recalls, "There was an enormous sense of pride and achievement. There were tears, this hugging thing going on ... they were exhausted."

With all this emotion related to the ending of the unit, it was considered very important to "de-role" and give a sense of closure to the experience. Children were invited to pretend they were holding a big heavy book that told the story of their experiences over the 7 weeks in the fictional company. Time was spent reflecting on the whole process: reading from the "book" and looking at pictures. Then one by one children wrote a final comment and symbolically "closed the book" on the learning experience. The "books" were placed on an imaginary shelf, where they could be lifted down and revisited at any time.

Throughout this unit, individual children showed initiative in spontaneous ways that demonstrated their sense of ownership and agency within the unit. Here are some examples:

- One girl made a paper briefcase, which she brought to every meeting.
- The same child drew up a petition on behalf of the protesters and passed it around members of the company.

- A child in the class with special needs took responsibility even though she didn't always want to be fully involved in the company. She created her own independent study of Kaimanawa horses and shared it with the group. She also became very involved in the questioning of Gay in role as the DOC representative.
- One of the boys in the class took it upon himself to signal for quiet when the level of noise in the company got a bit high.
- A very quiet child sent an unprompted email to Viv, which was written in role as Penelope and gave suggestions for websites the company might look at.

Examined closely, these examples reveal not only a sense of self-efficacy and entitlement, but also a highly developed degree of metaxis (dual awareness of fictional and real worlds). This special feature of drama—the way it creates a dual reality—is one of its most potent aspects. As Bolton (1985) and Edmiston (2003) remind us, children are able to hold the "as if" world of the drama alongside the "as is" world of their real lives. Then, as they work in the fictional world, children learn to take risks in safety, grapple with and solve problems and gain valuable insights that inform their real-world understanding. They also get opportunities in the "as if" world to take on higher status than the real world might afford.

In this unit, evidence of children's increasing sense of their own status was seen in the way their vocabulary became sophisticated and adult-like. Children adopted the language that was being modelled and frequently used statements such as, "Do any of the colleagues wish to add a comment?" or "I fear I may have offended a colleague." Another reason children may have sought to use adult language and concepts was because of the high status and complex matters being discussed (see Whyte, Fraser, Aitken, & Price, 2012). Children were positioned as being as capable as adults when they were confronted with the multiple perspectives on the Kaimanawa issue and trusted to be able to cope with these. Lynette recalled some doubts about whether the children would cope:

> Initially I wasn't so sure they would make that shift. They were so pro horse at first. When Gay first arrived in role as the DOC person, they were quite hostile and showed an unwillingness to listen—but the more they researched the more they could see both sides. Viv obviously knew they could do it but I wasn't convinced they could take the adult perspective and see the complexity.

The children themselves had some insights into how they felt about being treated as adults. In written reflections on the learning journey, some children remarked that this way of working had set them up for intermediate or high school. Another student noticed how the repositioning changed relationships between the children themselves:

> The MOTE [Mantle of the Expert] gave room 10 a chance to be 'adults' for a day. It was really interesting to discuss and be with people in the class when they are being adults because it was very different then [*sic*] when we are doing work normally.

The same child was also able to see a change in her relationship with actual adults through the process: "Because everyone is treated equally it is amazing when children and teachers alike all come together to work."

As already described, the planning and implementation of this unit of work was a highly collaborative affair. Lynette worked closely with Viv and Gay in the planning phases, and Viv and her student-teachers also participated in classes once a week as part of their university course about Mantle of the Expert. For Lynette to open her class up in this way depended on high levels of trust and careful communication between all parties.

Lynette also called on the visual arts expertise of an academic colleague to supply specialist knowledge in storyboarding. Lynette commented:

> We could have done it another way I suppose—through Google or something. But for Graham to actually be there was great. I'm all for this use of outside experts. I highly recommend to other teachers to have someone in to develop their skills and step them through the process ... He gave them examples, he gave them camera shots, a huge amount of support in photography. I thought they'd use a lot of images from the internet but a lot of them ended up using photos of freeze frames around the school environment.

Lynette and the company maintained their contact with Graham after the professional development visit. Graham was able to offer advice and answer questions, and the children enjoyed sending him their finished work. This sense of having a real-world audience for their work (as well as a fictional audience—the client) seems to have motivated the children's sense of purpose even further.

A striking feature of this unit was the way students took responsibility for the quality of their own work. Evidence of quality control was seen in the amount of time children took to revisit and refocus their work. The groups undertook up to four redrafts of the storyboards without being told to do this by the teacher. As already mentioned, children took work home and worked on through the lunch hour and before school. In Lynette's words: "Children functioned at a high level. They set high standards for themselves." Children recognised this about themselves. One child wrote on her reflection, "Doing my jobs well is something that I am compelled to do and it is so amazing when my team mates help me achieve that."

A key moment in terms of self-moderated "quality control" was when the children opted to bargain with their fictional client over the number of storyboards they could reasonably produce. Lynette recalled:

> They felt the time restraints wouldn't allow them to do more than two storyboards of quality. They got back to the client and re-negotiated the conditions of the commission. It's wonderful—they didn't want to compromise their standards.

In a sense, this moment is evidence of the opposite of reaching out for outside advice and quality assurance. The advice on quality comes from the children themselves, and is offered as advice for the outsider!

Links to curriculum

What follows is a copy of Lynette's planning showing curriculum learning areas covered within this unit (levels 2, 3 and 4).

Social Studies

- Understand that events have causes and effects.
- Understand how formal and informal groups make decisions that impact on communities.
- Understand how people make decisions about access to and use of resources.

Science

- Investigating—ask questions, find evidence, explore simple models and carry out appropriate investigations to develop simple explanations.

- Explore knowledge when considering issues that concern them.
- Explore various aspects of an issue and make decisions about possible actions.
- Ecology—explain how living things are suited to their particular habitat and how they respond to environmental changes both naturally and animal induced.

Maths

- Measurement—use linear scales and whole numbers of metric units for length, perimeter and area; find areas of rectangles; represent objects with scale drawings.
- Statistical investigations—conduct investigations using statistical enquiry cycle: asking questions, gathering, sorting and displaying multivariate category and whole number data and simple time-series data to answer questions.
- Identify patterns and trends in context.
- Communicate findings using data displays.

Health and Physical Education

- Personal identity—describe how their own feelings, beliefs and actions and those of other people contribute to their personal self worth.

Drama

- Developing ideas—initiate and develop ideas with others to create drama.
- Present and respond to drama, identifying ways in which elements, techniques, conventions and technologies create meaning in their own work and others' work.

English

Listening, reading, viewing
- Structure—identify a range of text forms and recognises some of their characteristics and conventions.

- Processes and strategies—integrate sources of information and prior knowledge with developing confidence to make sense of increasing varied and complex text.
- Ideas—show a developing understanding of ideas within, across and beyond texts.
- Make meaning of increasingly complex text by identifying main and subsidiary ideas in them.

Speaking, writing and presenting

- Ideas—select, form and communicate ideas on a range of topics.
- Language features—use a range of vocabulary to communicate meaning.
- Use oral, written and visual language features to create meaning and effect and engage interest.
- Structure—organise texts, using a range of appropriate structures.

Assessment of learning in these curriculum learning areas was carried out through ongoing formative conversations. In addition, certain assessable items were produced as part of the journey (scale drawings, written discussions, statistical displays, storyboards, final presentations, children's own reflections and self-assessments on their work in relation to the key competencies).

Key competencies

Children were challenged to extend themselves in all five of the key competencies during this unit. Certain competencies took prominence at different stages of the unit, as follows.

Thinking: During the preparation of arguments for the storyboards, children grappled with ethical and philosophical issues well beyond their level. They were challenged to think through and appreciate both sides of an issue.

Managing self: This competency was tested throughout, but perhaps most of all when children worked under intense pressure in groups preparing their final presentation.

Participating and contributing: Children's participation and contributions were valued and tested in the immediate world of the classroom and the fictional context of the company. Children also explored how people contribute to society as scientists and protesters.

Using language, symbols and text: The unit encouraged children to explore written, oral and visual languages and also to decode messages and explore features of the voice in meaningful contexts.

Relating to others: This competency could be seen as the crux of this unit of work, both in terms of children relating to each other within the class and in terms of the task itself, which had them grappling with two strongly opposing points of view on an environmental issue. As Lynette noted:

> Something important the children learned was to stand back from the story. They didn't have to take a personal stance or position themselves within the storyboards. I think they learned to be impartial. From swinging from one position to another they came to a point where it was possible to see both sides.

What Lynette is describing here is the capacity for empathy. The ability to see a situation from a range of perspectives is an important social skill, allowing children to think flexibly (Costa, 2008). Perhaps even more importantly, empathy is the basis for moral thinking and ethical integrity for children, and indeed all human beings. Neelands (2001) and O'Connor and Dunmill (2005) make a case for empathy being the single most important competency for human beings in the modern world.

Conclusion

The aim of this unit was to challenge children to debate an ethical issue related to animals and bio-ethics. Assessment evidence showed that all children achieved this to a high level, both individually (within their written work) and collectively (in the joint presentation). The children developed an understanding of the complexity within the Kaimanawa horse issue and were able to juxtapose and honour two points of view. Evidence of the sophisticated level of children's understanding can be found, ironically enough, in their lack of engagement with a storybook Lynette tried to introduce to them:

> We were going to introduce the storybook [*Kaimanawa Princess*, by Dianne Haworth] but in the end I didn't go far with this as it didn't engage the children. The author presents a very one-sided view of the issue and children

were uncomfortable with that given their own knowledge and embracing of the complexity.

As well as being very satisfied with the meta-curriculum learning, Lynette was pleased with the quality of learning in maths, science, English, social science and drama that happened through this unit. This quality was maintained by her careful short-term micro-planning within the overarching unit plan and her opportunities for support from Viv and Gay. Lynette found learning to plan "on the hoof" was quite challenging but ultimately rewarding:

> For teachers starting out the scary thing is you feel you are not owning it—you don't know where you are going next. Every day after school I'd be thinking 'Where are we going next?' But it's actually great. As long as you have the support with the planning phase ... Or to put it another way, you come to realise you are owning it *more*—you are right inside it. You become more caught up in it. I think that's the beauty of it.

Lynette also commented on the strengthened relationships between the children in the class. Much of the work was done in small-group formations, where children were left to form their own groups on the basis of interest, rather than being teacher-selected on the basis of ability. Lynette considered that the students' relationships within these groups and within the class as a whole were respectful and valuing. Children who might previously have been on the outer seemed to be seen by their peers as valued members of the company:

> There seems to be a want to listen, and take on everyone's ideas. More able children led the others, delegated and empowered others to share their ideas. There's definitely more input from the children who are often disengaged.

In their reflections on the unit, the children had some suggestions for what might improve the experience in future. These included more opportunities to work outdoors and more opportunities to research and present ideas as individuals rather than in groups. The level of engagement and enjoyment reported by the children was high in every case except one. The child who reported difficulty was absent at the start of the unit and struggled to develop the "buy in" to the company as well as experiencing some tensions within his storyboard group. This raises implications regarding the importance of continuity and how teachers can ensure all children build belief.

Lynette's only note of caution about the whole process is that it was somewhat tiring for children to work at such a level of intensity. While she was impressed with how engrossed children became in the learning, she did wonder if the class would have been able to sustain their energy levels if the unit had gone for any longer than 7 weeks. None of the children raised this as an issue, but it may be something for teachers to bear in mind when considering using a similar approach. However, any unit that engrosses children at this level is bound to require focus and energy, all of which makes for an engaged and motivating experience. A sense of fatigue is aligned with satisfaction about a job well done—a job that was worth pursuing in the first place.

References

Bolton, G. (1985). Changes in thinking about drama in education. *Theory into Practice, 24*(3), 151–157.

Bolton, G. (2003). Dorothy Heathcote's story: Biography of a remarkable drama teacher. Stoke on Trent, UK, & Sterling, VA: Trentham Books.

Costa, A. L. (2008). *The school as a home for the mind: Creating mindful curriculum, instruction and dialogue* (2nd ed.). Moorabbin, VIC: Hawker Brownlow.

Edmiston, B. (2003). What's my position?: Role, frame and positioning when using process drama. *Research in Drama Education, 8*(2), 221–229.

Education through drama: Planning with Heathcote. (n.d.). [DVD recording] New York: Insight Media.

Heathcote, D. (1984). Signs and portents. In L. Johnson & C. O'Neill (Eds.), *Dorothy Heathcote: Collected writings* (pp. 160–169). Cheltenham, UK: Stanley Thornes.

Heston, S. (n.d.). *The Dorothy Heathcote archive.* Manchester: Manchester Metropolitan University. Retrieved from http://www.did.stu.mmu.ac.uk/dha/hcheston.asp

Ministry of Education. (1997). *Social studies in the New Zealand curriculum.* Wellington: Learning Media.

Ministry of Education. (2007). *The New Zealand curriculum.* Wellington: Learning Media.

Neelands, J. (2001, December). *11/09: The space in our hearts.* Paper presented at the 2nd International Theatre and Drama Education conference, Athens.

O'Connor, P., & Dunmill, M. (2005). *Key competencies and the arts in the New Zealand curriculum.* Retrieved from http://nzcurriculum.tki.org.nz/Cu...e-New-Zealand-curriculum-Word-88KB

Whyte, B., Fraser, D., Aitken, V., & Price, G. (2012). Interactive group activity: A socially mediated tool for opening an interpretative space in classroom research. *International Journal of Qualitative Studies in Education.* DOI:10.1080/09518398.2012.725140. Retrieved from http://dx.doi.org/10.1080/09518398.2012.725140

CHAPTER FIVE

Creating an Interactive Museum

Barbara Whyte with Coryn Knapper

Introduction

Coryn works in a large urban multicultural school that comprises over 50 different ethnic groups. She is a very experienced teacher (over 40 years working in primary classrooms), with strengths in teaching the arts, particularly music and drama. From her own account she was revitalised by attending a Mantle of the Expert conference in Hamilton in 2009 and subsequently put what she had learned into practice in her classroom teaching. Her Years 5/6 class had been on school camp at Waitomo at the beginning of 2010 and developed knowledge about caves and tourism. On returning to school the class completed a Mantle of the Expert unit about water sports, during which they formed a company called "WAI", abbreviated from the full title of Water-sports Adventures Incorporated. Coryn said the follow-on unit, which is described here, "arose out of that earlier experience".

The children had been fascinated by the caves and thoroughly enjoyed the blackwater rafting activities within the caves. Coryn capitalised on their heightened interest to initiate a social studies unit about life during the Stone Age. In line with the approach used by the other teachers in the syndicate (described in Chapter Six), the unit was to be contextualised within a Mantle of the Expert drama with a keen orientation to the arts. The Mantle of the Expert approach is differentiated from open-ended inquiry because of the way the teacher carefully plans some aspects while letting other tasks arise naturally from developing events (Aitken,

2009). Therefore, Coryn skeleton-planned and tailored the Stone Age unit specifically for the learners within her own class, and with an arts bias, but anticipated that responding to the children's ideas as the unit evolved would require flexibility and perhaps deviation from this original planning. Negotiating method and content as the children encounter authentic tasks and solve realistic problems resonates with contemporary integrative curriculum practices, and also aligns with *The New Zealand Curriculum* (Ministry of Education, 2007).

The big idea

The big idea, "That we remember and conserve the past in many ways", was the umbrella concept that encompassed the integrated unit. The key questions for the unit developed from this concept were:

- How do we remember or find out about the past?
- Why do we remember the past?
- What do we need to know about people from the Stone Age to create an interactive exhibition?

Fig 5.1 *Girls explain their museum display*

The hook

Coryn established the new Mantle of the Expert with the pretext that a group of children blackwater rafting in caves (one of the water-sport activities of their company, Water-sports Adventures Incorporated (WAI)) had come across some old cave paintings that were then identified as originating during the Stone Age. The class investigated resources such as books and websites of cave paintings of the world, including the Lascaux cave paintings in France. They came to the realisation that, where cave paintings had been discovered in the past, tourists had damaged them by visiting the caves, and so the concept of "needing to avoid damage" or preservation was extremely pertinent for the children. When the owners of the island (where the cave paintings were discovered) indicated that they wanted to create a museum based around the cave paintings, the children's WAI company responded with informed interest and empathy.

The WAI company's rationale for the museum was based on two factors: first, it was possible interested people may not always have the capacity to cope with the physical demands of blackwater rafting in order to gain access to the real paintings; and second, if large numbers of tourists did enter the caves to see the paintings it was likely they would damage the fragile cave environment and the paintings would deteriorate. The company argued that if people could view replicas of the cave paintings in a museum, they could also learn about the lives of people who lived during the Stone Age through activities and displays. This rationale stimulated the WAI company to commission Coryn's class (in effect, an old company commissioning a new company comprising the same children) to design and create interactive displays for such a museum. This commission was accepted by the class and provided the sense of purpose for the unit. The task from there was to create such a museum for others to learn from and enjoy.

Organising for learning

Having replied to and accepted the commission, the class then set about forming a new company that could carry it out. The children spent time in groups negotiating the name and logo of the company. In consideration of the commission and the necessity to incorporate an arts focus, Coryn steered the direction towards the notion of artists/performers. The company name generated by the children that proved most popular was Realistic Artists and Performers (RAP).

At this stage the children needed to establish their identity as company personnel by writing a company biography (bio). This kind of writing was first modelled by the teacher, composing her own fictitious bio as the company manager. This was followed by the children writing their own bios as staff in the company, collaboratively creating a bio/history of the company as one that had expertise in creating exhibits. Such writing within a meaningful context furthered the school and classroom literacy goals.

The class then decided on what initially needed to be done to fulfil the commission and came up with a basic list of tasks that encompassed finding out about: cave paintings in general; the life and times of Stone Age people; and interactive activities in museums. Creating this collaborative task list represented the beginning of co-constructed planning between class and teacher. It was Coryn's belief that the children needed a core understanding of background knowledge before they could plan for the commission task with authenticity, but she also knew they needed to be motivated to engage with that knowledge. She felt collaborative planning enticed the children at this stage of the process and created a basis on which to build the children's general knowledge. Cook (1992) identifies how effective the process of collaborative planning can be to engage the initial interest of learners in a class project. Coryn facilitated the base knowledge development of the class by drawing on a range of curriculum areas (instances are described below) in order to expose them to certain information she knew they needed.

For example, for visual art the children researched the topic of cave paintings in order to be able to create a set of paintings of animals in this style that would be replicas for the museum. For literacy, reading groups studied material that contained stories set in the Stone Age era. The groups followed up their reading with tasks that required further research using a range of media (e.g., Internet searches and story-summarising comic-book making). From the start of the unit Coryn also regularly read chapters aloud from a novel, *Scorched Bone* (Ford, 2008), about a tribe living in the Stone Age. During the reading she frequently highlighted an event in the novel with dramatic strategies in order to differentiate perspectives and to highlight dilemmas and tensions for the characters in the story. Thus when Coryn assumed a role as a senior tribe member, it became the signal to the class for some children to adopt the roles of named people in the story while the rest became the collective "tribe".

Fig 5.2 *Coryn in role as a senior tribe leader*

As the children became more informed, Coryn also utilised specific dramatic conventions such as freeze frame and role on the wall (see Ministry of Education, 2006, for descriptions of these) as part of the shared reading, to focus closely on characters living in the Stone Age setting. Drama devotees Kana and Aitken (2007) and Heathcote and Bolton (1995) argue that the ways in which drama builds empathy and understanding are central to drama's purpose. It is clear this purpose drove Coryn as she helped the class develop appropriate core knowledge for the unit:

> I could get the arts out of most things, but why I like using drama is it gives 'a sense of involvement and I am part of it'. When you go into drama, you take on a role and become part of the events as they are happening. This is why I like using it a lot because the kids can instantly relate to a story if they've been role-playing parts of the book or using other drama techniques. They can think 'Ah—this is part of my life—I've lived part of this' when it comes up. Drama helps live it, [and] therefore gives a sense of involvement.

Deepening the learning

Once the children's knowledge base about the Stone Age had expanded, Coryn refocused the unit back on the interactive museum and the commissioned task. Coryn acknowledged that this phase of the study really promoted co-constructed planning and greater input from the children. Earlier the children had brainstormed the kind of knowledge about Stone Age people they thought should be shown in the museum and came up with their own questions about this era. The questions encompassed how Stone Age people travelled, how they coped when sick or injured, how they communicated, and how they dealt with death. From there the children grouped themselves into teams centred on a particular key question, collaboratively worked out ways of locating information to find out answers and allocated investigative tasks to each member.

However, Coryn felt they needed prompting to delve deeper into the commissioned task and contemplate the range of people who might visit the museum. In her view, teams were aware of topics younger children might be interested in, but they also needed to consider what constituted age-appropriate activities suitable for teaching these topics. The interactive museum aspect of the commission required teams to broaden their research projects to include different types of activities, as well as the facts needed to answer questions about the Stone Age.

It took quite a few sessions to complete this section of the unit. The class spent valuable time drawing on the collective strength of the children's knowledge and ideas. There were, for example, frequent "stop and share" sessions that communicated what teams had created so that children could get ideas from their peers. However, a need for the teacher to guide some aspects remained:

> I still needed to support by going into role as the RAP company manager, formally modelling a position as facilitator for the children's sharing sessions, with statements and questions such as, 'Would this team please report on what has been done since the last meeting', 'What do you think you need to do now?' and 'Could another team please give suggestions to this team of what they could do now.' But it was not long before the teams soon started doing these things by themselves.

Some individuals in the teams needed more input from the teacher. In order to foster quality learning, Coryn made sure team talk focused on the question 'Have we done everything we need to do to fulfil the commission?' So, whenever the children did anything as a company member or employee, the children "stepped into adult shoes" as commissioned staff members. This positioning of the children as adults was frequently manifested in the language level used by children. For example, one child identified herself as a "computer geek" during a classroom conversation but described herself as having "a degree in computer animation" when in role within the company.

After extensive team processing and planning, the museum exhibits were created in a "hands-on" phase of the unit over 2 weeks. The interactive exhibits included:

- two "choose the right answer" plays/skits: one about two Stone Age hunters hunting an animal, in which their styles are compared (the first hunter botches it so the animal escapes, while the second hunter does the kill "properly"); the other about making fire with sticks (the first fire-maker burns herself, while the other makes fire safely): the audience needs to select the "right approach" for each scenario and state why it was chosen
- a jigsaw puzzle (involving a large, hand-drawn image of a Stone Age village scene)
- a "feely bag" puzzle (which contained handmade Stone Age artefacts)
- a physical game of "Spear the Sabre-tooth Tiger" (a target game generating points, using hand-crafted pumice spearheads on stick spears)
- a question-and-answer book (e.g., "Guess the animal's name from the cave painting")
- a sequential wall exhibit (of papier-mâché reconstructed Stone Age hunting tools, using associated read/feel/write activities for each tool)
- an interactive computer quiz about the Stone Age (utilising a PowerPoint presentation).

The list above looks relatively straightforward, but the 2-week exhibit-making process was far from problem free. There were plays to script, cast and practise; costumes and props to make, sort and store; materials and resources to source, organise and share; constructions to create, move and safeguard; decisions to be made, unmade and negotiated; and deadlines to be planned, met and stretched. It was a complex period during the unit and entailed many disputes and struggles for resolution. The key competency of relating to others was thoroughly tested. It was a focused learning-by-doing time and, although the teacher was readily on hand, the children were encouraged to solve their own dilemmas and issues in the manner of company staff members.

Fig 5.3 *Children making Stone Age artefacts for their museum*

Eventually the exhibits were ready for the interactive museum. A Year 4 class, invited to "visit, view and do", was expected one afternoon, and the commissioned company had planned a preview and run-through for earlier in the day. The museum teams set up less vigorous activities within the classroom space (puzzles, quizzes and wall activity) and more vigorous activities outside (plays and the spear-throwing game) ready for the afternoon visitors. In anticipation of this preview and run-through, and in collaboration with Coryn's Mantle of the Expert mentor (drama lecturer Viv Aitken), an intervention was introduced into the unit. The mentor went into role as a museum apprentice, Jordan, from Auckland, who had earlier sent a letter to the RAP company expressing interest in seeing their interactive museum. A return letter from the company invited her to visit when the exhibits were ready. Jordan's visit was scheduled for the morning of the official dress rehearsal, and she appeared at the door when a RAP company meeting reviewing team progress was in action.

Excited by Jordan's arrival and welcoming her as a meeting participant, the children then got back to the meeting business of reporting on their team's interactive activities. There was honest critique of these activities by peers, and possible pitfalls were challenged and justified. One debate about the quiz booklet having answers at the back of it prompted ethical debate (What if the children read the answers instead of thinking about it themselves, i.e., cheat?) and learning debate (Does it matter if they do read the answers, because they will still be learning?).

After the meeting ended, teams demonstrated their activities to each other. Jordan was invited by the sequential wall-exhibit team to trial their activity. She did so as though confused about how the exhibit worked, generating lots of questions which the team attempted to answer. To help clarify it, the team suggested Jordan pretend to be a child working her way through the exhibit. This would allow the team to practise their supervisor role for the afternoon session and explain the what and how of the activity.

Fig 5.4 *Trying out the jigsaw activity*

When it was time for the class to re-convene as a company, Jordan commented on the museum exhibits and asked for useful ideas to take back to Auckland. Jordan's role as a novice was clearly signalled, and her request to the class to give her advice was predicated on the fact that they had more experience than she did at making a museum interactive. Such a request underlined that the children as company personnel were to "give advice to a fellow adult".

Positioning children as capable knowers is a strategy used in Mantle of the Expert, which, among other benefits, reveals authentic ideas and understanding. The following transcription indicates that the children had garnered both pragmatic and philosophical learning about what constituted an engaging museum for children:

> Girl 3: When you're making an exhibition some ideas are very challenging to make [interactive]; really tough—but in a good way.
>
> Boy 4: So don't expect it to be easy.
>
> Boy 5: Children get bored easy ...
>
> Girl 4: If you're doing it on Early NZ, try to make it as real as you can.
>
> Boy 6: What she means is, try to make it as it looks like, for real—then [in that era]!
>
> [The bell goes for lunch. Four children decide to stay and give further advice to Jordan.]
>
> Girl 3: Don't call them games; call them activities—it's more important ... Museum people need to be friendly, know what they are doing, making it fun. Not just telling people all the answers. It's funner for me to learn and find out—most kids really want to learn, so they go out and find the answers themselves rather than just being told...
>
> Boy 2: Adding on to Michica [Girl 3]—it needs to be like that for adults too. When you think about it, if it's interactive you want to do it more.
>
> Girl 3: Practice makes perfect!
>
> Boy 2: If you learn the topic, you'll learn how to solve it [make it interesting].
>
> Girl 3: And ... go to the children themselves ...

Jordan expressed surprise at the contrast between the children's interactive exhibits and the no-touch policy of the museum that she worked for in Auckland. (This point was developed further when Jordan sent another letter to the class, thanking them for their hospitality and urging them to write to her manager to convince him that interactive displays were really important to children, which they duly did.)

Coryn noted that her class really enjoyed being in the role of supervisors when helping the younger children with the exhibits later in the afternoon. Initially, the younger class was put into small groups and allocated to one exhibit. After completing the activities at that first exhibit, they were able to move on to any of the exhibits, but were assured of continued help from eager museum "staff". Sharing with the younger class provided an opportunity for the older children to demonstrate what they had learned, because it is Coryn's belief that "One of the best ways to learn is to teach others. You have to think hard about it to take others through it." Coryn is in good company here, as the research on peer tutoring emphasises that when you teach something, you learn twice (see, for example, Topping, 1994).

Some adaptations to original activities to accommodate younger learners and physical space were evident: the play/skit performers gave the audience a set of closed questions before they started, pre-warning they were going to check for answers at the end (which they did); the pumice spearheads "didn't work", so the spears were used without them; and the sequence wall activities were read aloud when there were too many of the younger children on site at one time to have individual turns. The visiting class provided oral feedback on the exhibits when requested by team members (such as speaking the words more clearly in the skits), who took the advice seriously and noted down comments for future reference.

Coryn hypothesised that by assuming adult roles (e.g., during the novel-reading role-plays, or researching as a company employee, or being an exhibition supervisor or a teacher at the interactive museum), children are enabled to better understand different perspectives, or more sides, of an argument. Nuthall (2007) also argues that we need to give children sufficient time on a project so that they "experience the information in different ways so they can crisscross the intellectual landscape from different angles" (p. 161). The different roles the children took within this unit enabled them to revisit concepts and ideas, which is central to deepening learning.

Coryn likes using Mantle of the Expert with multiple groups operating at one time, because it enables differentiation of the curriculum to meet diverse learning needs. As well, the key competencies (team work/

relating to others; persistence/managing self) come to the fore. It is her view that "content is less important than the process of going through it ... what/how ... and an outcome such as 'How will we know we've achieved it?'"

Having said this, Coryn also appreciates that content learning was engaging for the children. The excitement of learning information about the Stone Age is captured in one child's response to a query:

Researcher: Why did they bother making so many drawings of animals?

Girl: We've got that in our PowerPoint! See here: 'They would paint animals before they went hunting as a good luck charm. They would often put a handprint as a kind of signature.'

Researcher: Did you know this before?

Girl [emphatically]: No, none of it!

Fig 5.5 *Girls check their PowerPoint quiz*

As new ideas are opened up, Coryn says she appreciates the way children can follow their passions, interests and own lines of inquiry, noting, "There's lots of learning going on … which will reveal itself at some point!" She also values the peer teaching that those with special interests are able to carry out with other children. When asked what they had learned during the unit, two children piped up:

> Girl 2: I've learned heaps about computers. Marama [Girl 1] taught me how to do links to slides and do 'correct' or 'incorrect' when they make their choice [from the multi-choice options in the quiz].
>
> Girl 1: I'm a computer geek!

Coryn made time to bring everyone back together on a regular basis to share experiences and learning. She also thinks it is important to take time during the unit to take stock to ensure conceptual understanding is not being lost in the quest for information. Therefore, approximately halfway through the Stone Age unit she checked that the children were aware that people living during that era needed the specific interest items they were studying in order to survive.

She also used class mat gatherings in a similar way for summative assessment. For example, she noted that the unit "wrapped up fairly quickly" once the museum exhibits had been tried and tested, but later the class returned to discuss the big idea underpinning the study. She was pleased with the class response, which showed that the children understood that the interactive exhibits were different ways to record the past. But she was more satisfied when they were able to link how interactive exhibits and setting up a museum was "a way to help us remember the past".

Interactive Group Activity (IGA)

An interactive group activity (IGA) strategy in the TLRI research project that followed units of study showed the extent and nature of children's learning in the above unit. Five children (representing a cross-section of academic ability, gender and ethnicity) were pre-selected by the class teacher to participate in the strategy. During the IGA process, the five selected children would retreat with two researchers to a large empty classroom. They would then sort a jumbled selection of 25 images and

25 words specific to the Stone Age unit (but also including some random nonrelated images and words) into an arrangement that represented their agreed mutual understanding of the unit. The children were invited to add and remove words as required, and the experience was framed as "assisting" the interested but confused researchers, who were unable to make sense of their data without help. While the completed array of images and words decided on by the children illustrated a summative understanding of the unit, it was the rich dialogue elicited and recorded during the task that revealed the extent and quality of thinking about aspects of the unit.

Each time it was used in the research project, the IGA task engendered considerable physical movement and lively interaction and debate (some quite heated) as the children energetically sorted and arranged the images/words over approximately an hour. The experience was characterised by negotiation, collaborative conversation and engagement, and in the researchers' view the IGA tool promotes a sense of learning as contestable, provisional and emergent.

Transcriptions of discussion by Coryn's group of five children suggest this group of children went through a process replicating that followed by other groups in the same project. That is, they started with literal interpretations of the images and words in the early stages of the array-making, and moved towards more complex and abstract conceptual understanding and connection-making. The vital process is illustrated in the following description and transcript clips as the children's conversation goes back and forth when they contemplate and debate meanings.

After initial matching of words to images, the children tried variations of method in their sorting and arranging. The example below shows that when the children came to the insight that words could be grouped under headings, they began to think more globally by adding new words that represented wider conceptual understanding. The following extract reveals this phenomenon as the children debate what constitutes learning. In essence, they have started to theorise about epistemology:

S3: I reckon we could get lots of words that only cover one thing—and then that could come under other things, under other main big ideas.

R2: Could you give us an example?

S3: So ... over there we have shaman—that could be tribe, because tribe would come under more things than just shaman.

S3: I reckon a big word could be constructing because they're con ...

S1: Yeah, that's actually a really good word—constructing.

S2: Yeah constructing—they're building.

S4: They're not just building things, they're building their brains. They're learning new things. They don't actually know much about the Stone Age, 'cause they've learnt that. What we've been told is, that animals are hunted for food and clothing.

S3 [interrupts]: I reckon you should put a thing that says learning.

S1: Yeah, but we have some people in the photo who aren't learning.

S4: Everybody is learning. We are learning because we're teaching little kids, so we're learning how to tell kids about what we've learnt. And they're learning, because we're telling—they're learning how to paint Stone Age things, make spearheads, do some jigsaw puzzles, so ...

S1: Learning is putting things in your brain and remembering it so in later life you can do something with it.

A child writes "learning" onto a blank word-card, which prompts added vigorous debate among the group, but also motivates a further child to resort to a metaphorical model to express her understanding and convince others of her hypothesis:

S1: I think we should have one big idea. We should have to decide on one big idea.

S4: Jab in the middle—smack jab in the middle [slaps 'learning' down in the centre].

S1: But listen! It's a bit like the solar system [rapidly draws an image on a card that shows 'learning' in the centre of a cloud with 10 box shapes surrounding the cloud and wiggly lines from the boxes to the cloud and from box to box creating a concentric ring effect].

Fig 5.6 *Using the interactive group activity*

The transcript clips above show that the children's learning is not just occurring in teacher-created logically organised boxes, but extends through peer-mediated debate. The debate is often productive, but it also contains what Elley (1996) refers to as "irregular spurts, sidetracks, inconsistencies and misconceptions" (p. 12). The researchers believe the IGA contributes to Twist and McDowall's (2010) concept of "interpretative space" (i.e., not just one right answer) by fostering rich conversations for all partakers, other than just those who frequently tend to dominate group interactions. (For more about the IGA process, see Whyte, Fraser, Aitken, & Price, 2012.)

Links to curriculum

For Coryn, flexibility is the key for a teacher to utilise Mantle of the Expert as integrated curriculum, and to respond to where children might want to take a unit. She warns, "You may set out with one intention but that's not the way it goes if you follow the kids. You have to be prepared to let go of something you've planned." However, she appreciates the way the two approaches complement each other: "Being able to jump into one or the other [Mantle of the Expert and curriculum requirements] is part of the flow of teaching in this way." During a Mantle of the Expert programme, children engage over time in activities that are both curriculum tasks and tasks that would be professional practices in the fictional enterprise. As well, one of seven elements mandatory in sustaining a Mantle of the Expert approach is to engage the curriculum firmly and at relevant levels (Heathcote & Bolton, 1995). It is clear from the following list that a variety of curricula was engaged with during the Stone Age unit.

Social science

Social studies is the most obvious curriculum learning area in terms of the context and content of the unit, and is self-evident in the paragraphs above.

Literacy

Coryn said that, like most teachers, she anticipates where scaffolding might be required through knowing the children's capabilities and needs. An example during the Stone Age unit was that she was watching for the right place to revisit and refine paragraphing skills. Coryn noted that:

> It came up three times: first, when the children wrote factual reports about what they were learning; second, about half way through the unit, when I was checking they had a conceptual grasp of what Stone Age people needed to survive; and later, when teams were planning their interactive exhibits.

These three instances are detailed and explained here.

Writing: structuring writing/paragraphing
- The first instance occurred within the genre of information reports, using a single item and a single explanatory paragraph; for example, state why Stone Age people needed animals, fire, weapons, stone etc. to survive and provide reasons why, for that item.
- The second instance was as a concept check, again in the context of information reports, but using a single conceptual statement and multiple explanatory paragraphs. For example, state the big idea "Most Stone Age tribes were nomadic and food was hard to find", and give whole-paragraph reasons for several comparative points to support this statement, such as: needed animals to survive and why

(food, skins for clothing, warmth and shelter); fire was important and why (cooking, warmth, light, fending off animals/marauding tribes); stone was very useful, and in what ways; wood was useful, and in what ways.

- The third instance was in the team planning sheet, when the children were starting out on the interactive aspect of exhibits. Team members stated what their exhibit was and the required materials, described what it taught about Stone Age people and justified why their exhibit choice was "interactive".

In addition, paragraph writing was reinforced when integrated with persuasive writing, after Jordan sent a letter to the class indicating she had reported on her visit to their museum to her Auckland museum manager. Unfortunately, wrote Jordan, the manager seemed to believe children should not be allowed to touch anything in a museum. The children were very indignant and, prompted by a request from Jordan, wrote persuasive letters to the manager countering his attitude.

Descriptive writing
The teacher modelled, and the children subsequently created, a collaborative company biography and wrote their own "bios" as company personnel.

Formal writing
This included letters; for example, an invitation to Jordan in response to her request to see the museum.

Reading for information/nonfiction and fiction

This involved library display books: novels read as required reading (independently read text). Daily reading groups studied content about the Stone Age. One group of children did guided silent reading (independent); two children did reciprocal reading (with the teacher).

Visual language: Comic-book stories

These were created as summaries of key points in novels read as "required reading". Children could independently create a comic-book story. However, the two children doing reciprocal reading with the teacher were guided through their comic-book activity.

Associated skills throughout unit

These included dictionary and spelling skills.

The arts

Drama

Mantle of the Expert included:

- forming a class company and assuming company roles
- story reading, including teacher-in-role, students-in-role, process drama conventions of role-on-the-wall, and freeze-frame.

There were also plays/skits scripted and performed for an audience, by the children.

Visual art

Replica animal cave paintings were produced by the children in accurate style for the museum.

Dance

During story reading there was a whole-class re-enactment of "the kill" after a tribe returned from the hunt (with drummer accompaniment).

Technology/Information technology

Computers

Children researched on the Internet and created a PowerPoint presentation for one of the museum interactive exhibits. The teacher utilised the computer with an interactive whiteboard for negotiating (e.g., the vote for the logo that clearly and succinctly showed the company idea), and for creating an effective interactive resource to illustrate a timeline showing the Stone Age as dates, and moveable images using EasyTeach software. Coryn promotes the value of the interactive whiteboard for helping to keep track of the unit as it progresses and for simplifying teacher record-keeping.

Conclusion

Coryn has a philosophical stance that values student contribution and agency, and this comes through strongly in the research findings and in her classroom practice. A lot of the time she is willing to stand by these beliefs and let the interests and ideas of the children lead aspects of the classroom programme. This stance was evident in the Stone Age unit described above, which was obviously a time when the children took responsibility for a sizeable proportion of what went on during the study once the basic groundwork had been established by the teacher. However, Coryn is honest in stating that there are frequently times during the year when this approach can be too time consuming. On such occasions, she takes a more overt leadership role in planning and leading a classroom unit.

She is, as indicated earlier, an advocate for using a Mantle of the Expert approach because of the way it naturally integrates the curriculum and fosters student contribution and agency. In this unit, an integrated approach facilitated critical inquiry; that is, conscious consideration of ethical implications and consequences. In the view of Ackerman and Perkins (1989), integrated curriculum approaches introduce children to the meta-curriculum, which they believe transcends the explicit curriculum and leads children towards the ability to learn, reason, solve problems and make independent decisions. Such abilities and decisions appeared to be demonstrated at differing levels by children in this class as they proceeded through the integrated Mantle of the Expert unit and developed a conceptual grasp of how people lived in the Stone Age. In Coryn's view:

> MOTE gives a clean slate upon which you can express what you want to say or show, particularly from the child's side. A teacher has always got at the back of their mind the curriculum and requirements—so not such a clean slate. Children don't consciously have those requirements upon them. They know there are expectations and ideas they are focusing on, but they have more freedom than the teacher to absorb big ideas.

Coryn also takes time to incorporate the arts, which are her passion, but tries not to force fit them if it is not appropriate. She is a legend in the Waikato district for her capacity to lead school music programmes, but it was noticeable that music was the one area of the arts curriculum that Coryn did not try to incorporate into the Stone Age study. She said that music did not fit naturally into that study, so she left it out and focused on drama because the unit utilised a Mantle of the Expert approach. She added:

> I do feel strongly the arts should be taught separately in their own right. In MOTE the children are mainly using what they already know. Another time I would perhaps start them with stand-alone arts lessons, such as music skills, and the children could then bring that learning into a MOTE.

However, she was receptive to a later suggestion from a colleague that music could have been introduced during the Mantle of the Expert as professional development for the staff of the company, so that background music could have been created and incorporated into the museum exhibits.

It is evident that one of the features of Coryn's classroom practice is her skill in questioning, and she stood out in the research findings as a teacher who consistently asked genuine questions. That is, the questions she regularly asked encouraged children to think in depth, rather than being perfunctory, closed or superficial. The combination of quality questioning and an integrated curriculum approach through Mantle of the Expert seems to have provided Coryn with an appropriate vehicle to take her class back in time to comprehend how life was lived in the Stone Age.

In the process of creating exhibits that could help teach others what they had learned, the children journeyed across learning terrain that developed key competencies such as managing self and relating to others (Ministry of Education, 2007). It helped lead the children to a deeper understanding of how items such as interactive exhibits in a museum can be a way people remember the past. As a result, the children were able to offer informed views about the characteristics of child-friendly museums from the reality of their own experience from the unit.

Reflecting on the advantages of the Mantle of the Expert approach, Coryn indicated an intention to further build on what she had learned from this unit:

> Thinking about next year (my final year of teaching!): we might form a company that runs an art museum, like the Waikato Arts Museum, and we could create various static/interactive/video displays throughout the year on whatever topics we are studying. I like the idea of the same company throughout the year as the kids really buy into the company idea and we can have a different focus each term. We can also find out about our museum and what it does for the community.

Polk (2006) suggests that "It is the teachers' responsibility to grow as practitioners, stay current in their field, and continually evolve as professionals" (p. 23). It would seem that Coryn exemplifies teachers who continue to evolve as professionals, even in the final years of their teaching careers. It is clear that even a highly experienced teacher such as Coryn has found it stimulating to continue to develop her pedagogy by adopting Mantle of the Expert and other curriculum integration approaches late in her career.

References

Ackerman, D., & Perkins, D. (1989). Integrating thinking and learning skills across the curriculum. In H. Jacobs (Ed.), *Interdisciplinary curriculum: Design and implementation* (pp. 77–96). Alexandria, VA: Association for Supervision and Curriculum Development.

Aitken, V. (2009, 3 July). Mantle of the expert. *New Zealand Education Review*, p. 10.

Cook, J. (1992). Negotiating the curriculum: Programming for learning. In G. Boomer, N. Lester, C. Onore, & J. Cook (Eds.), *Negotiating the curriculum: Educating for the 21st century* (pp. 15–31). London: Falmer Press.

Elley, W. 1996. Curriculum reform: Forwards or backwards? *Delta, 48*(1), 11–18.

Ford, V. (2008). *Scorched bone*. Auckland: Scholastic.

Heathcote, D., & Bolton, G. (1995). *Drama for learning: Dorothy Heathcote's Mantle of the Expert approach to education*. Portsmouth, NH: Heinemann.

Kana, P., & Aitken, V. (2007). "She didn't ask me about my grandma": Using process drama to explore issues of cultural exclusion and educational leadership. *Journal of Educational Administration, 45*(6), 697–710.

Ministry of Education. (2006). *Playing our stories*. Wellington: Learning Media.

Ministry of Education. (2007). *The New Zealand curriculum*. Wellington: Learning Media.

Nuthall, G. (2007). *The hidden lives of learners*. Wellington: New Zealand Council for Educational Research.

Polk, J. (2006). Traits of effective teachers. *Arts Education Policy Review, 107*(4), 23–29.

Topping, K. (1994). Peer tutoring. In P. Kutnick & C. Rogers (Eds.), *Groups in schools* (pp. 104–128). London: Cassell.

Twist, J., & McDowall, S. (2010). *Lifelong literacy: The integration of key competencies and reading.* Report prepared for Cognition Education Research Trust. Wellington: New Zealand Council for Educational Research.

Whyte, B., Fraser, D., Aitken, V., & Price, G. (2012). Interactive group activity: A socially mediated tool for opening an interpretive space in classroom research. *International Journal of Qualitative Studies in Education.* DOI:10.1080/09518398.2012.725140 Retrieved from http://dx.doi.org/10.1080/09518398.2012.725140

CHAPTER SIX

Mining Learning

Deborah Fraser with
Michelle Parkes and Whakarongo Tauranga

Introduction

School camps are one of the most memorable experiences children have from their years of schooling. In order to capitalise on camp experiences, teachers foreground the trip with preparatory activities and devise follow-up work on return from camp that seeks to deepen children's learning. This chapter outlines the innovative follow-up integrated curriculum work that occurred in two Years 5/6 classrooms.

The initial camp experience comprised a visit to the Waitomo caves, staying at the Tokikapu marae. A range of learning experiences were focused on, including cultural and historical issues plus the examination of cave fauna and limestone formations. The knowledge that children developed through the shared camp experience was an ideal platform for building further learning through integration. The children's enthusiasm and engagement were added reasons for pursuing a unit emanating from the experience.

As teachers will recognise, here was great potential for expanding the unit; in essence, "the teachable moment". The teachers appreciated the potential of this to deepen the learning for and with the children. Deciding on the Mantle of the Expert approach was a strategic decision, because it not only fosters inquiry processes but also "makes links within and across learning areas" (Ministry of Education, 2007, p. 9). As discussed in Chapter Three, Mantle of the Expert involves children taking on the role of experts in an imaginary enterprise. It also encourages children to wrestle with complex issues, resist premature closure, deal with ambiguity and take an ethical stance.

Whakarongo and Michelle are experienced teachers in a large, urban, multicultural school which comprises over 50 different ethnic groups. They both have an abiding interest in integrated curriculum and were aware that too often such units of study revert to teacher-driven thematic approaches. After attending a drama conference on Mantle of the Expert, they were motivated to try this approach with their Years 5/6 classes. Mantle of the Expert provided them both with an approach to integration they had not previously experienced. It also introduced them to a range of dramatic strategies they could incorporate in their teaching.

The big idea

The major focus of the integrated unit was to discover ways to preserve New Zealand's natural heritage. The challenge was for the children to consider not only ways to preserve the environment but also to educate present and future generations. Complicating this was the necessity to take seriously the issues surrounding preservation of natural caves and the contrasting needs of mining and capitalist development. These tensions and contrasting viewpoints were a major aspect of the study and spearheaded the need to deepen investigation.

The hook

Fictional letters are often used as a provocation within Mantle of the Expert, providing a catalyst for engagement and hooking children into an issue. In both classes the hook comprised a letter from a fictional character who commissioned the class to utilise their expertise to preserve and develop a cave area. This set up an ethical tension because it encouraged children to consider preservation of the cave and education of the public alongside development of the area. The conscious use of dramatic tension provided a paradox that evoked a fertile context for learning. The following fictional letter provides an example.

A similar fictional letter, crafted by Michelle, was used in her class to hook the children in. In her case, the letter was ostensibly from the father of a

652 Sparkle Road
Waitomo

Friday 4 June 2010

Dear Ms. Tauranga,

My name is Anthea Glow and I am writing to you with the hope that you and your class may be able to help my family.

Our property is situated on a hill and according to public record it was once a pa site but is now our lifestyle block surrounded by native bush. Recently we discovered an opening hidden in the bush that led to an underground cave. The cave is a treasure trove filled with creatures such as cave weta, spiders, bats, glow-worms, eels and koura. There has even been some evidence that moa may have roamed this place. It is truly an amazing sight. The caves have an abundance of beautiful stalactites and stalagmites that appear to be millions of years old. A renowned speleologist has told us that our cave is one of the largest cave systems discovered in recent times.

We understand that your class have some experience and knowledge of caves such as this, after your recent trip to Waitomo and subsequent investigations into the cave creatures that lived there.

Our family is interested in protecting this very precious part of New Zealand's history for future generations to enjoy. We have had increasing interest in our cave, with various school groups, and tourist companies requesting tours and information about the cave and surrounding landscape.

We believe that your class may be able to help us develop the site in a way that is environmentally friendly and also enables us to educate people that choose to visit our cave. It is of the utmost importance to us that the landscape is protected from damage. We are also concerned that large numbers of tourists may have a negative impact on the creatures that live in the cave.

We would welcome your considered suggestions for how we might best develop this sight into one of New Zealand's leading local attractions. We have discussed as a family the possibility of opening a museum and visitor centre but are unsure what form this may take. We would be interested in any designs that you had to offer.

We look forward with great anticipation to hearing from you. I will be in Hamilton on business on Friday the 12 of June and would love to meet with you to discuss any initial concepts that you may have.

Kindest regards

Anthea Glow.

large extended farming family who had discovered a cave on his property and wondered if it should be made available to the wider public. Using Mantle of the Expert enables teachers to take artistic licence like this, playfully crafting letters they know will challenge and entice the children.

Organising for learning

As a result of the commissions the letters invited, the classes formed their own companies. As outlined in Chapter Three, the forming of a company, enterprise or collective identity is part and parcel of Mantle of the Expert. The children thought long and hard about a suitable name that encapsulated their imagined company. A number of names were suggested and a class vote was taken to choose the most popular name. Whakarongo's class chose Environmental Property Resources (EPR) and Michelle's class chose Aotearoa Caving Experts (ACE) as their respective company names.

The children then set about developing the culture of their company. What sort of company were they? What did they represent? What was the history of their work to date? What were some of their previous commissions and the particular highlights of their work? All of these questions involved them in devising a fictional timeline of work, including specific stand-out projects. In this way the children were "building belief" in the values, skills and aims of their company. Central to the ethos of the company as it developed was its high standards of integrity. This was reflected in a logo and company motto devised by the children that emulated their company's vision. After much debate the motto for EPR was decided upon as "If you can imagine it, we can manage it", and for ACE the motto was "We go back in time to safeguard our future". The teachers were impressed with the high level of discussion amongst their children as they devised a suitable, pithy motto that best represented their company values.

Discussion ensued in each class about what it meant to be ethical. What would this mean in their practice? The children investigated ethical dilemmas through role plays, weighing up what was right in a variety of circumstances. For example, in small groups they debated and contrasted using cheap hardwood of dubious origin from a local importer (which would save them money) with a renewable building source that would be more expensive but not sourced from depleted rainforests.

To further build belief, the children designed their own company ID badges. This again reinforced how the fictional world gives licence to act as if it is real. Real company executives have ID cards and this signifier engendered a sense of pride and efficacy. On the ID cards were identity details, including name, address, contact numbers, email and job title. In Michelle's class they also made their own security swipe entry for company members as they came into the classroom. Discussions about job titles culminated in the crafting of more detailed job descriptions: What did they do in the company? What was their specific role, and how did it facilitate the company's aims and values?

Deepening the learning

A variety of job roles were decided upon, which required the children to research what the jobs entailed. The jobs in Whakarongo's class included:

- architects (of the museum and café)
- gift shop souvenir designers
- café menu designers
- visitor information centre
- playground designers
- landscape designers
- security
- museum cashiers
- advertisers.

This diverse range of job roles brought some challenges and required the children to seek outside support and guidance. Each group contacted real-life outside experts in their respective fields in order to ascertain the details of their jobs. The children set up a functioning company email account and started corresponding with various community experts to help them with their tasks. A few of the children held meetings at the school (e.g., to interview an architect). This required the children to initiate and take responsibility for meetings. The example below is one of the many ways children expressed their agency.

Children's email to the school office

> Dear office ladies,
>
> Our names are Tama, Peter and Akash and we are expecting a visitor tomorrow.
>
> His name is David Anderson and he will be meeting us in the office at 12.00 pm.
>
> We have booked MR1 from 12.00–1.00 pm.
>
> Kind Regards
>
> Tama, Peter and Akash

Later on the same group sought feedback and advice from this real architect (a school parent) on their initial plans. This ongoing relationship enabled a real need-to-know basis for the children's questions and problems. It also enabled the children to think carefully about aesthetics, environmental impact, sustainability and all the things their company stood for. The architect sent the class some photographs of buildings that fulfilled the company's criteria and that were carefully considered when designing their own museum layout.

Fig 6.1 *A selection of the architect's photos*

Another fruitful invitation was made to one of the university staff, who was asked to discuss design issues with the menu designers and advertisers. Graham Price (an art educator and researcher) worked with the children on their concepts, their audience, their priority and the specific nature of the tasks required. He commented that the nature of the conversation he had with the group was very different from the usual teaching guidance one might give to a group of children. For a start, it was initiated by the children. Second, the intent was to discuss design issues and not just be shown what to do. Finally, as a result, the quality of the discussion was more like a conversation between peers.

Fig 6.2 *Two girls scrutinise their brochure design, which advertises the museum and visitor centre. After consultation with Graham, they decide to use more "spotlight" words. These included: "funtabulous", "sparkling", "dazzling" and "glowing". It also advises children to bring old clothes, as the outside activities are such that "you get dirty-birty".*

Each of the job groups was also required to negotiate success criteria, which included a series of logical steps needed to accomplish their tasks. Over time it became apparent that the next challenge was to co-ordinate all these job roles into one cohesive plan or aim. At a board meeting of the company the children developed an overall concept for the museum and the visitor centre using Microsoft Word drawing tools to consolidate the working plan. This became the basis of a three-dimensional model, made to scale, which encapsulated their design for their client, Mrs Glow.

In Michelle's class the children chose their own specialty focus within the company and formed research groups based on shared interest. These groups included entomologists, palaeontologists, speleologists and chiroptologists. In order to understand more about their expert roles, Michelle organised resources such as National Library books and electronic resource material with which the children engaged. The children's Internet searches further supplemented their investigations. The children delighted in discovering scientific facts such as the location of a wētā's ears and how glow worms generate bioluminescence.

Fig 6.3 *The chiroptologists' research team poster*

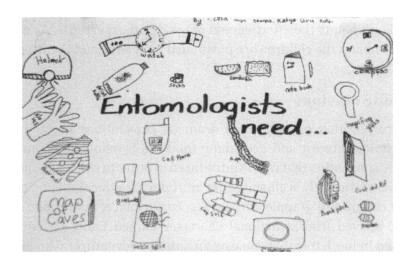

Fig 6.4 *The entomologists' research team poster*

A number of cave fauna were also created by the children, combining study and visual art skills.

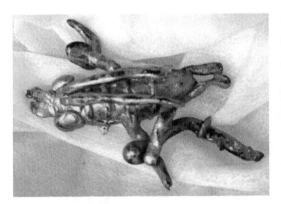

Fig 6.5 *Plasti-clay cave wētā*

Michelle commented that:

> You can give the kids the power and it's up to them if they accept it. If they feel ownership then that's the difference. They become passionate. I've done a lot of inquiry learning and they are strong in that but there is often one group that is a bit off, not quite bought in. With Mantle it's the use of role play and stepping into a company that empowers learners at very different levels. They self-select the tasks and buy into their own goals.

Michelle pinpoints the effectiveness of taking an expert role. As experts in the company, the children are positioned as agentic and their research has real purpose.

Symbolic tensions

The incorporation of well-timed dramatic conventions has the effect of sustaining interest and deepening thinking. Symbolic tensions are a dramatic convention that can be introduced in order to challenge children. They are particularly well suited for introducing ethical dilemmas that require children to grapple with issues. For instance, in Michelle's class a letter arrived from a fictional character named Cathy Cavener. She explained in her letter that she was an outdoor adventurer who enjoyed caving and abseiling. She also enjoyed collecting mementoes of her escapades, including a carved rock she found in a cave and now uses as a doorstep. She asked ACE if they would like some of the other relics she had collected over the years for their museum. This letter had the desired shock effect on the children and they expressed their concerns about Cathy Cavener's misguided and naïve behaviour.

Normally, children would be wary of expressing anger and dismay at an adult's actions. The fictional frame of the drama, however, allows participants to explore and push boundaries in the imagined world while remaining assured that their actions will have no consequences in the real world. Bolton (2003) identifies the importance of this safe frame, both for safety reasons and to deepen learning:

> Tasks are and must be fictional … at a level there is a 'no penalty' awareness felt by the doer, a sense of freeing the individual, so that they find themselves 'caught off guard' into identifying skills they did not know they had. (p. 136)

The children were not at risk in any way when expressing indignation towards Cathy Cavener and "calling" her on her unethical and anti-environmental actions. In fact, the process gave them licence to stand up for what they believed without the fear of censure or criticism. In such cases, power is democratically vested with all who participate in the classroom. The power children hold in this example is not illusory; it is made palpable by their investment in the issue at stake. Dramatic conventions like this can deepen children's commitment and learning. The children went on to write their own narratives for the objects they had made for their museum, inventing circumstances for how they came to be there and exploring the ethics of museum collections.

Whakarongo recruited the assistance of another teacher, Gay Gilbert, to embody the tension that would hopefully challenge children's thinking further. An initial email was received from Gay in role as Mrs Dea Mond, the (fictional) CEO of a precious gems jewellery company. Her email requested a visit to the company to make her pitch for a business arrangement that could be of mutual interest. The company agreed to her visit, which took place later that same week. During her visit, Mrs Dea Mond made it clear that she would like to take some core samples from the cave to check the chemical composition, because she suspected it contained gems such as diamonds worth millions of dollars. If so, the mining of the cave would be a profitable endeavour for all concerned, creating jobs for the local town and a ready source of income. This symbolic tension presented the children with a dilemma: should they succumb to the lure of profit and the tangible benefits of job security, or should they consider the wider environmental and ethical issues at stake? The children asked Mrs Dea Mond a series of questions about her intentions.

After her visit they decided to hold a town meeting to discuss the proposal. This meeting required them to consider the groups within the town who may have a vested interest in the possible mining of the cave for fiscal reasons (e.g., the local pub owners, the supermarket, real estate firm, clothing stores, hardware stores, garages). Prior to the meeting the children created an argument based on the perspective of the person they had chosen to represent. This was an ideal focus for the teaching of argument writing, one of the school's literacy goals for the term. The company's ethical stance was one of preservation and protection, and so this argument was presented. However, there were others who represented the interests of town members outside the company and who were obliged to take alternative perspectives.

Consideration of opposing points of view like this required the children to think more deeply about issues than they may have done if the conservation line was the only point of view. The town meeting allowed for the airing of competing and contesting views emerging from Mrs Dea Mond's proposal. Such tensions are a catalyst for justifying stances and entertaining diverse perspectives rather than leaping to premature conclusions or viewing issues as black or white, right or wrong, good or bad. Children could see that there were factors and concerns whichever view was taken. In other words, the complexity inherent in the fictional task was akin to the complexity of debate about issues in the real world.

A vote was held and a letter written by two of the children to Mrs Dea Mond on behalf of the company:

Environmental Property Resources

28 Environmental Way
The Grotto
Waitomo
Phone: 0800 EPR EPR
E-Mail: epr@environment.co.nz
Web: www.epr.co.nz

3 September 2010

Dear Mrs Dea Mond,

Following our town meeting, which took place on the 2nd of September from 7:00PM to 8:30PM seven people agreed to accept your proposal to mine our cave. They agreed because they thought it would make more money for them.

However, 18 people declined your proposal. The majority of people said if mining took place it would harm the environment. If your company found lots of gold and gems you would continue to dig deeper and it might go to the museum and the museum would have to be shut down. Tourists would not like fake trees or fake stalagmites and stalactites either.

We want to thank you for your proposal but as representatives for Mrs Glow and her family, E.P.R have decided to decline your offer of mining on their behalf. It would not be in the best interests of the environment or the recent development of the museum and visitor centre.

Yours sincerely,

Taija and Jay

E.P.R Consultants

Transformations

For Whakarongo, it appeared that the children became more aware of their individual responsibility within the context of larger social settings such as the class, the company and the wider community. Their growing agency as learners was evident as they "stepped into adult shoes", taking increasing responsibility for their work. She commented:

> The thing I like the most [about Mantle] is I almost feel, on many days, surplus to requirements …

> I think it's about the fact that they are secure in the knowledge of what they are doing; they have a role; they know where they are heading and they have permission [to go there] …

> … more so with this because, in some ways, there is less direction by me than there are in other subjects … there is the expectation that they will be able to solve their own problems … to be the leader of your own destiny.

There was evidence of transformations for a number of children throughout the unit. For example, a shy, risk-averse girl made the following unsolicited comment to her teacher:

> When I was talking with Sue [Viv in role] I felt like an adult. I felt generous; I felt like you [points at teacher]. I felt like I was helping her. Yeah [bouncing up and down on the spot]! I liked feeling like that. I want to feel like that more often.

Another graphic example came from an unexpected event during the town meeting. A boy in the class who has autism took on the fictional role of a miner who wanted the mine to go ahead because it was his job and he would have no job and no money if it was not mined. Then later he became an environmentalist and stated, "I am concerned that the mine might be open cast and turn out to look like Martha [a mine in Waihi]. Would you like to see some photos on my laptop?" He then stood up and went to use his teacher's laptop. She whispered to him that this was imaginary, so he came to the front and pretended to open his imaginary laptop, typed on his keyboard to bring up the photos, and then held up his laptop so that the people at the meeting could see his photos. He then explained the photos and pointed to areas of interest. He "showed" the class photos of the mine, mine workers and protesters. It was clear to see the satisfaction on his face as he realised that he was pretending to be someone else with a pretend computer.

The teacher aide who was the boy's learning assistant and respite carer since he started school at age 5 said that it was the first time that she had seen him use his imagination in this way. People with autism can often be perplexed by the pretend, the fictional and the metaphorical. It was powerful to witness the disruption of this stereotype as he pretended to be someone he is not, let alone pretended to have a laptop that no one could see. The sustained opportunities to work in both the real and fictional worlds provided him with the chance to become more than the limits of his autism diagnosis. Viv, as visiting researcher to the class, asked what the children had learned about designing a museum and visitors centre. He offered the comment that "You need to have the love of something and if you have the love of what is important, it will be easy."

Early on the children appeared to undertake the various activities because they needed to be done, but a shift occurred when the children participated in the work of the company because "this is who we are and what we stand for". It was noted in this and other Mantle of the Expert examples that a significant turning point came when the children's (and teacher's) language changed from *I* to *we*, reinforcing that this was a project *we* were forging together.

Challenges and benefits

It is challenging for children to work this way. In effect they are stepping into adult shoes and participating as if they are experts. One could question the extent of this expectation for primary-age children. However, when asked this directly (in the research project), children can be very perceptive about the benefits, as the following dialogue between the first author and a Māori boy in the class reveals:

D: So what do you think you have learned from being in the company?

B: How to be an adult. How hard it is.

D: So why would you bother then, if it's hard then and you're still a kid?

B: You learn! Things like design ...

D: Well what's your role in the company?

B: I'm a museum architect. I did the main layout of the visitor centre.

The boy's comment resonates with research on children's learning about what makes for a quality education:

> Learning real, difficult, meaningful things, in collaboration with others, with some responsibility for determining how they go about it: this is exactly what young people themselves say they want. (Claxton, 2008, p. 94; see also Rudduck & Flutter, 2003)

In Michelle's class, the children gradually transformed their entire classroom into an interactive museum that fulfilled their initial client's commission. In planning for this, they held company meetings to identify and discuss the qualities of a good museum. The children's comments included:

> Instead of just things in display cases people could interact ... do things with exhibits.

> Try to keep the reading simple and let the public touch some things. Writing information is important, but not too much.

> You should pick something you are interested in but might not know much about ... so you can find out and discover more. If you are not interested in what you are making then it's going to show through to the public.

> It's like the speech I'm going to make. You have to have attitude, care about what you are doing.

> It's like buying a toy for your best friend ... you would have to choose something you were interested in, that they might like as well.

> Caring about the public is how you get good feedback.

These comments reveal their sense of audience and the importance of commitment. As they stepped into the job of creating a museum, they reflected on what it meant to educate people in ways that matter. The completed class museum, which was the culmination of the unit, revealed a range of displays and exhibits that educated the public about the unique fauna and formations that comprised the cave. It also highlighted the historical, cultural and environmental significance of caves and our responsibility as the present generation to preserve such unique areas for the future.

The children invited their parents to visit their museum, taking them through the various scientific, cultural, historical and aesthetic displays. It was evident from their hosting of this event that they had taken responsibility for the project. The children also wrote unsolicited comments in their school reports about their learning during the integrated unit. Michelle did not direct them to write about their Mantle of the Expert experience; she simply asked them to record what they had been most proud of over the year. The following comments were typical.

> What I am proud of is my carving. It took me so long and it ended up being a very realistic replica of a real taiaha.

Fig 6.7 *Child's carving*

> I am proud of my work in the Mantle of the Expert. In this it feels like I have taken huge steps forward in every area of my learning.

> I am proud of creating our class cave. I wanted my mum and dad to see how well I had done in everything this year. I made a rolling TV. It was special because it told people information about bats.

> I was a Palaeontologist. I learnt all about fossils and why they can be so valuable.

> It was so much fun showing the parents around our museum and telling them all about our carvings, the bats, weta, model pa sites, moa and all the other exhibits we had made.

> I am proud of our class museum. I think we put a lot of effort into making it work and no one complained about staying in three hours while parents walked around.

These comments indicate ownership and engagement. Further data collected reveal a number of observable engagement incidents. For example, of the 26 children in Whakarongo's class, every child talked about their company and their activities within it, outside of the integrated unit (e.g., during physical education or mathematics). For most of the children this happened many times. All but one of the children complained when they had to stop or were interrupted from their work in the company, and 24 of the 26 children asked for more work during the unit.

Engagement in class activities is an undeniably important component for students, and can be conceived as a means to an end as well as an end itself (Willms, 2003). Engaged students tend to participate more in class discussion and extracurricular activities; associate with the values, practices and goals of the school; be aware of the relevance of their schoolwork to their own lives; have better relationships with their peers and teachers; and be less likely to drop out of school and more likely to enrol in tertiary education (Finn & Kasza, 2009). Genuine engagement in school fosters social relationships and a sense of purpose, factors that directly affect many aspects of a student's life (Klem & Connell, 2004).

Fig 6.8 *Designers in the EPR company*

The data also showed the high volume of interactions occurring in any one classroom. In Michelle's class, for instance, there were 355 interactions between her and the children in a space of a 60-minute observation. This is not unusual in the busy life of contemporary classrooms. What is more significant is the quality of those interactions. Michelle used a number of stems and comments that were empathic and encouraging. These included:

- It is hard. You've found this very challenging …
- I'm just wondering …?
- Could you explain to me …?
- The reason I like the stream might be different from yours; what's yours?
- I want you to do what you think is best …

The comments and questions invite children to explain their reasoning, or ponder alongside her, or take responsibility or identify that learning is sometimes hard. Good learners know that learning can be hard, and they enjoy the struggle that comes from wrestling with ideas and making decisions, even if those decisions are not always the best (Claxton, 2002). Learning is not just the tidy solving of problems but also comes from taking risks and considering the outcomes.

Links to curriculum

Clearly, these integrated units assisted children with "becoming connected and actively involved" (Ministry of Education, 2007, p. 8). It also prompted them to consider just what sort of future they wanted. As guardians of the cave environment they were obliged to find ways to preserve it and educate future generations. This reflects the curriculum vision to "secure a sustainable … and environmental future for our country" (p. 8).

Planning for such units requires both subtlety and explicitness. For example, Michelle commented on the explicitness needed as well as the negotiation required to ensure children have a say in the what and how of learning:

> My children all know our broad forward planning. It's a visible document to them on the classroom wall. This is where we've come from … this is where we might go towards. They know I'm open to their contribution and they earn the right to suggest changes of direction.

Whakarongo commented on the subtlety required behind the scenes for this kind of planning for learning:

> It's like a really good dress, all the best bits are hidden … all the structure is in behind it … it's absolutely crucial; you need those bits in place for the rest of it to work.

The specific curriculum links to learning areas were as follows:

- Drama: practical knowledge, developing ideas, communicating and interpreting (level 3); for example, roles activated through job descriptions, visitors, tensions, town meeting
- English: speaking, writing, presenting (level 3), which included:
  - integrating sources of information, processes and strategies to identify, form and express ideas
  - showing a developing understanding of how to shape texts for different purposes and audiences (e.g., argument writing)
- Visual art: applying knowledge of elements and principles, and a variety of materials and processes, to explore some art-making conventions (level 3); for example, creating sandstone tools modelled on those used by early Māori, papier mâché pā sites, construction of hard-cover myth and legends books, plasti-clay cave wētā
- Science: living world (levels 3/4): life processes, ecology, understanding, investigating and communicating in and through science
- ICT: a class Gmail account, used by the children to contact community members and set up meetings; solving design concept challenges using drawing tools in Microsoft Word.

The connections to the key competencies were as follows:

- thinking: imagining, abstract problem-solving, reasoning, estimating, measuring, predicting, reflecting, designing, manipulation of materials and images
- managing self: listening, meeting goals and deadlines, reaching professional standards of work, working to success criteria
- relating to others: collaborating to create a company name and mission statement, debating ethical dilemmas, imagining selves as company members
- understanding language, symbols and texts: choosing images and text for advertising, menus, designs, logo, persuasive writing, creating a company timeline and job roles

- participating and contributing: contacting community members, arranging meetings, taking the initiative, taking a stance, using their knowledge about issues of concern, participating in democratic voting and decision-making procedures.

Conclusion

It is clear that children have no problem with blurring the real and fictional worlds. Indeed, for children in particular, engaging with the fictional has its own "reality" akin to that which we perceive to be real (Edmiston, 2003). O'Toole (1992) recognises the tension between the real and the imaginary worlds as inherently productive. Mantle of the Expert enables them to "develop more understanding about a facet of life" (Edmiston, 2003, p. 222) through immersion in the imaginary. In many respects, the potential of the fictional world for extending learning is greater than the real. As Kupperman, Stanzler, Fahy and Hapgood (2007) state:

> The outcome of the World Cup matters a great deal and at the same time not at all. It allows a complete investment of energy, and an opportunity to take risks, knowing that in the end, it's just a game. (p. 166)

Being a company and designing a museum and visitor centre is just a game, but a game that matters in ways that encourage children to work hard and push boundaries. The fictional realm offers children the chance to act as experts in their chosen fields. And the responsibility that goes with such expertise includes doing research, considering client needs and creating a quality outcome. Permeating their work is the need to be ethical, which means decisions require careful consideration of the values the companies espouse.

Designing museums and visitor centres for clients provides an avenue to reflect children's care for the environment. While they had concern for the entertainment and educational value, there were also emotional and spiritual concerns. The dismay and discussion evoked by Cathy Cavener's letter and the debate during the town meeting revealed a range of strong views. In Whakarongo's class their final letter reveals the reality that democracy does not always entail consensus.

Whakarongo reflected that next time she would limit the number of job roles within the company because it became difficult to sustain what amounted to a range of mini-mantles operating within the room. Even though the children took increasing responsibility, limiting the number of jobs would help with managing the dynamics of the company and maintaining high standards. In many respects, less is indeed more.

Both teachers reflected on the immense amount of learning they had undertaken. This was only their second attempt at Mantle of the Expert, and while they had achieved a lot they were well aware that there was much yet to be discovered, developed and refined. They were concerned that the drama-for-learning aspect became lost at times and realised that they needed to build in dramatic conventions at strategic points. They also realised that the quality of children's thinking was enhanced with the introduction of well-timed symbolic tensions, as outlined above. Their own thinking was stretched by consideration of these issues. As deputy principal Gay Gilbert noted, "When you do a mantle you grow children, but you also grow teachers." It seems that this inquiry approach to integrated learning is highly motivating for both children and their teachers.

Fig 6.9 *At work on a company task*

Beane argues that schools should offer children more learning like this:

> The work they do should involve more making and doing, more building and creating, and less of the deadening drudgery that too many of our curriculum arrangements call for. (Beane, 2005, p. 136)

Viv Aitken as a leader in Mantle of the Expert has set up a support group for teachers in the region (see http://mantleoftheexpert.co.nz), and this continues to foster teacher development. It also builds a community of inquiry around Mantle of the Expert across schools and class levels. Sustaining any innovation in education relies on the commitment of teachers and is more likely to last when teachers have such a supportive forum with like-minded advocates, and when they experience first hand the benefits for the children they teach.

References

Beane, J. (2005). *A reason to teach: Creating classrooms of dignity and hope.* Portsmouth, NH: Heinemann.

Bolton, G. (2003). *Dorothy Heathcote's story: Biography of a remarkable drama teacher.* Stoke on Trent, UK: Trentham Books.

Claxton, G. (2002). *Building learning power.* Bristol, UK: TLO.

Claxton, G. (2008). *What's the point of school? Rediscovering the heart of education.* Oxford, UK: Oneworld.

Edmiston, B. (2003). What's my position?: Role, frame and positioning when using process drama. *Research in Drama Education*, *8*(2), 221–230.

Finn, J. D., & Kasza, K. A. (2009). Disengagement from school. In J. Morton (Ed.), *Engaging young people in learning: Why does it matter and what can we do?* (pp. 4–35). Wellington: NZCER Press.

Klem, A. M., & Connell, J. P. (2004). Relationships matter: Linking teacher support to student engagement and achievement. *Journal of School Health*, 74(7), 262–273.

Kupperman, J., Stanzler, J. Fahy, M., & Hapgood, S. (2007). Games, school and the benefits of inefficiency. *International Journal of Learning*, *13*(9), 161–168.

Ministry of Education. (2007). *The New Zealand curriculum.* Wellington: Learning Media.

O'Toole, J. (1992). *The process of drama: Negotiating art and meaning.* New York, NY: Routledge.

Rudduck, J., & Flutter, J. (2003). *How to improve your school: Giving pupils a voice.* London, UK: Continuum.

Willms, J. D. (2003). *Student engagement at school: A sense of belonging and participation: Results from PISA 2000.* Paris: OECD.

CHAPTER SEVEN

Te Mana, te Wehi me te Ihi: Teaching from Who We Are

Viv Aitken with Elicia Pirini

Introduction

Fig 7.1 *Elicia Pirini*

Elicia Pirini was the teacher of a Year 3 class within a special character Catholic primary school. The school was at the time 10 years old, with a rapidly growing roll of predominantly European students. Elicia is Māori, and when planning for this unit her aim was to work in a way that wove together stories and values from her cultural heritage with the spirituality of the school's character. Elicia chose to do this through the cross-curricula teaching approach of Mantle of the Expert (see Chapter Three).

The motivation for the unit arose from the schoolwide theme for the term, which was part of the compulsory overarching framework for religious education within the school. The theme was "God as creator and our relationship with creation", and Elicia looked for ways to manifest learning that would address this theme in conjunction with Māori cultural and spiritual conceptions of creation and tapu o te whenua—the sacredness of the land.

Fig 7.2 *The prayer table (with mauri stone)*

Elicia's initial planning style emerged from a brainstorm of key questions related to the theme, including: What is special about planet earth? What effects change the specialness? Why do places change? Who decides what's special and what's not?

Elicia also sought advice and input from other Mantle of the Expert teachers and made use of published planning tools (see www. mantleoftheexpert.com). Using Heathcote's list of "possible enterprises", Elicia brainstormed adult jobs that would connect children to these concepts of God's creation in a way that had personal relevance to them. She was very conscious of wanting to work with spiritual and ethical concepts but in a way that avoided "pat" answers from the children, and instead engaged with what the children really thought and felt.

Elicia's early planning ideas included forming a time capsule company (commissioned to send a time capsule into space to show what is important on planet earth), or taking on the role of mediators (commissioned to mediate the separation of Rangi and Papa, from the Māori creation stories). She also contemplated asking children to create an island adventure park giving visitors an experience of the wonders of creation, or becoming *National Geographic* photographers gathering images for a special edition of the magazine. In the event, none of these ideas were used, although they all felt fruitful.

Being open to multiple opportunities in the early stages allowed Elicia not to close down her options too early: "My advice to teachers, don't go with that first idea. By going wide you can go narrow later. You need to give yourself lots of time for this stage."

Elicia spent a lot of time at this stage of planning because she wanted to find the right entry point for her class, a large number of whom had learning difficulties and low literacy. "Nothing seemed right. I was worried that some of the concepts were a little too abstract for the age level. I knew where I wanted to go but I didn't want it to be out of reach for that group."

The big idea

The big idea for the unit landed when Elicia remembered a story *Koro and the Mauri Stone*, which she had once owned as a picture book:

> I was brainstorming Māori stories with environmental concepts and this one came into my head. It's a story that starts in the past in New Zealand—the environment is beautiful and unspoilt. Then development occurs—trees are cut down, birds go away. Koro can see that the whānau is falling apart and the people are not happy. He talks to the local community about the mauri stone and the fact that this place has lost its life force, or mauri. Koro tells the whānau that the stone needs to be found again. He builds a beautiful kite and where the kite lands, he believes this is where the stone is to be found.

This story became the pretext for the Mantle of the Expert exploration. But Elicia did not begin by telling the students the story. Instead, she put students into role as archaeologists as a way for them to explore the discovery of the mauri stone and gradually uncover the environmental aspects and the life force that it represents.

The hook

Elicia wanted to begin the drama by introducing the mauri stone as a mystery object. She put a lot of consideration into finding the right prop to represent the mauri stone, eventually choosing a clay pinch pot she had made during an art class.

Fig 7.3 *The 'mauri stone' pinch pot*

The drama began with the stone, which was delivered to the class by the teacher in role as a member of the community who had found the mysterious object on a building site. Elicia deliberately did not tell the children what the stone was because she wanted it to be a beguiling mystery. This use of clues and incomplete information can be a successful way of hooking interest and promoting inquiry. The children's ideas were very wide ranging. Some got very caught up with the fact that the object had a hole in it—perhaps it was a musical instrument? Some thought it was a kind of egg. One child suggested Elicia blow into the hole because, as he said, "I thought it would pop a leg out of the other side!"

Organising for learning

After the "stone" had been brought in and pondered, Elicia realised the class needed to develop their role as archaeologists. She helped them make this transition through inquiry questions such as, "What kind of people might get sent this?" and "What do archaeologists do?"

Elicia spent a substantial amount of time (2 or 3 weeks) building belief in the company, and with it some awareness of the profession of archaeology. This was done through a mix of real-world resources (such as clips of archaeologists at work) and imagined activities to build children's sense of themselves in this identity. The children came up with a company name, the Special Digging Company, and they created business cards and individual company profiles detailing their work in the company.

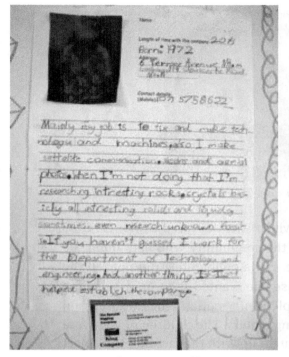

Fig 7.4 *Company profiles*   Fig 7.5 *Company business cards*

Elicia was able to use these profiles to fulfil a required task for an asTTle assessment.[1] The children also worked imaginatively with the element of dramatic space. They mapped their office space and physically rearranged the classroom furniture. They also established a sense of the company's past by creating a timeline of past digs and a company mission statement, and displayed these on the wall.

Classroom recordings taken at this stage of the experience show children beginning to accept their identity and position as experts in the imagined context:

> We're the extractors ... I carefully take it out without breaking it—I use something soft so I don't break it ... my dad works for a digging company. Once he found a really old bath tub. Really old—like my poppa. My poppa turned 100 on the 1st of May.

---

1   AsTTle stands for Assessment Tools for Teaching and Learning and it is an educational resource for the assessment of reading and writing, developed for the Ministry of Education by the University of Auckland.

Fig 7.6 *Special Digging Company offices*

The second part of this quote shows the child exhibiting the dual awareness of fictional role and ongoing reality, known as metaxis, which is a key feature of learning in drama. Edmiston (2003) suggests that operating in both the "as is" and "as if" worlds simultaneously encourages children to gain deeper insights as they reflect on both the real and imagined worlds and draw links between the two. The early stages of a Mantle of the Expert inquiry are particularly crucial for establishing this dual awareness, and one way the teacher can gauge whether this is occurring is by listening to the children's language. The use of "we" suggests an acceptance of a shared company identity, while personal comments linked to "I" may reveal an ongoing awareness of the student's social reality outside the company.

When Elicia had spent some time building the company identity, it was time for the commission to be delivered. Elicia did this through the convention of a letter delivered from the fictional client, a community group called Tapu o te Whenua. The letter described how the group was concerned about the development of a plastics factory on a piece of land. They had found a mauri stone (the one the children had already received) and they remembered the story that had been handed down. The writers of the letter felt that the land should not be developed for the factory but instead returned to its previous state. The letter commissioned the archaeologists to conduct an investigation of the land to determine whether it was of value and asked them to represent their findings at a forthcoming council meeting.

Elicia balanced the formal tone of the letter with a dramatic use of imagery to hook the children emotionally. She recalls:

> I remember we had a lovely 'Mantle moment' when I said, 'And now the land looks like this'—and revealed a photo of a desert-type setting. And the kids gasped ... You never forget those moments.

The children in role as archaeologists accepted the commission and started working out how to carry out their investigation.

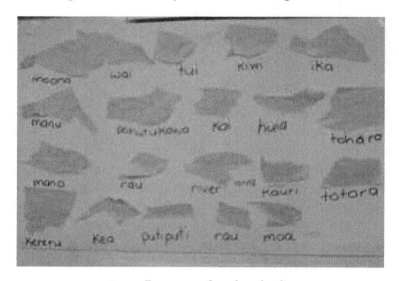

Fig 7.7 *Fragments found at the dig*

The first productive tension was introduced when the class received fragments of paper found at the site. The fragments contained words in te reo Māori describing animals and plants, and also the word "mano", which means "thousand".

Children translated the words using a dictionary and concluded that the words probably described the land before it had become desert. In what Elicia recalls as "another Mantle moment", one child suddenly made the connection, shouting out, "It's about before—there were probably thousands of fish, thousands of trees, thousands of everything!" Here once again, Elicia's preference was to introduce a clue with a sense of mystery to entice students forward in their thinking, rather than simply giving instructions or asking questions. This kind of deliberate withholding of information to raise levels of curiosity and the "need for information" is a significant feature of the Mantle of the Expert approach, as described by Heston (n.d.).

The class was asked what they should do next. One child responded, "We should go and look over the site and see if there's any [trees] left. We'll need to use the big machines carefully." This comment reveals how much for her the imagined world and her role as archaeologist had now been fully accepted.

Deepening the learning

At this point, Elicia recalled a *School Journal* story she had read in the past about Cook's naturalist, Joseph Banks, who commented in his diary about the deafening noise from bird sounds in the bush. Elicia was wondering how to link to this story when she took Viv's advice and went into role as Joseph Banks:

> Straight after that chat with Viv, which happened at morning interval, I turned round and went into role as Banks in the next lesson! I framed the words on paper as fragments of his diary ... and asked the children for help to reconstruct the missing diary.

By moving into role herself, particularly by taking a low-status figure as someone who needed help, Elicia repositioned the children in the class and raised their status. Bowell and Heap (2002) describe how this kind of repositioning can help teachers set up new possibilities for agency for children in the classroom:

> Because the usual hierarchy of the classroom is set to one side ... the way is open for the children to make a contribution to the shape and direction of their own learning. The teacher sidesteps her usual position of ultimate authority, final arbiter of situations and fountainhead of knowledge—especially when she chooses a role which is more vulnerable—so that the children are confronted with the decision-making, research, problem-solving and team working necessary to resolve the central dilemma of the drama. (p. 53)

In Elicia's case, the vulnerable role was that of Joseph Banks, and the dilemma was how to recreate his lost diary. The process of reconstructing the diary was carried out through close observational drawings of native birds and plants, done in pastel and in pencil. As these were completed, they were proudly displayed in the classroom.

Fig 7.8 *Pastel and coloured pen drawings*

Fig 7.9 *Observational pencil sketch*

Elicia recalls how engaged the children became in the task of drawing, and how the dramatic frame and the use of teacher-in-role gave the task extra purpose:

It was more than an art lesson—the purpose gave it extra intensity. I kept visiting as Joseph Banks and giving them scaffolding in role ... I'd put on his voice and say things like, 'Hmmmm. When I carried out my observations I would look very closely. What are you noticing about the veins? I see. Well, make sure you include that.'

Having met Joseph Banks through the teacher-in-role, children were intrigued enough about him to carry out their own inquiries into the real historical figure. One child suggested, "We might have to research more on who Joseph Banks was", while another added, "I might research him at home. Dad doesn't let me touch his flash history books but I can use the Internet." Some children did indeed go on to research the facts around Joseph Banks in their own time.

The reconstruction of Joseph Banks's diaries through visual art was hard work for the children, and Elicia admits the process felt a bit laboured at times. She wondered whether she was asking too much of a Year 3 class. In particular, she was concerned that "some of the lower level kids switched off". However, she was struck by how engagement levels with these children lifted whenever she went back into role as Banks:

It captured them. Felt really good ... Last year if I thought I'd lost them I thought, 'That's it, stop, do something else, let them out for a run', but now I'm feeling there are other ways of building engagement than stopping and going for a run! I learned I can recapture the engagement by going into another layer, pull them into the drama.

Elicia's decision to take on the role of Joseph Banks appears to have been a significant turning point in this unit. Taking on a role so spontaneously was a brave action, even for a teacher who had tried working in role before, and Elicia required a bit of encouragement to give it a go. She is not alone in this. Studies of teaching in role (Ackroyd-Pilkington, 2001; Balaisis, 2002; Bowell & Heap, 2002) invariably find that teachers are reluctant or nervous about moving into role, particularly when it involves the concept of sharing power with the children. However, the strategy represents such a potent combination of invitation, role modelling, repositioning and enablement that many teachers have found it well worth overcoming their reservations to make use of it. This was certainly the case for Elicia.

The repositioning of children as competent adults also seemed to have positive impacts on the children's behaviour. Having been quite a difficult class at times—"the first class to really challenge me in 20 years"—Elicia noticed a marked improvement in focus and respectful behaviour, appropriate to their role as adults with a serious job to complete. In a Skype conversation Elicia described the new sense of focus that she could see developing in her class:

> Stillness. I can feel the stillness in the room. Girls are crossing their legs and sitting upright because that's what adults do. More focus on the teacher when talking. Waiting for others to finish before speaking.

On one visit from the research team Elicia needed to redirect student behaviour but did so within the fictional frame, reminding the company about appropriate etiquette for a meeting. The sense of heightened engagement and purpose, leading to improved behaviour in the classroom, is commonly seen in units of work that use Mantle of the Expert and is attributable to the depth of belief established in the early stages of the work.

Elicia began to feel that although most of the class was fully engaged, the progression of activities the class was moving through was complex and not always easy for children to follow. The "flow" of the Mantle of the Expert work was also interrupted by whole-school activities and required assessments. Some children were unsettled and one child was having problems buying in at all because she had been away for some time. Elicia found that recording/scribing the journey the class had been on through words and pictures on the classroom walls really helped children to recap and to see their story progressing.

Elicia was particularly struck by the power of putting work on the wall:

> Mantle of the Expert is process orientated, but as I put the work up, it's powerful. Kids are really into seeing their stuff on the wall. They are proud of the result because of how they got to the product. It's like process and product are married somehow.

This visual storying was important for parents and other teachers too. Eventually, members of the board of trustees visited the room and saw the learning displayed on the walls.

It was about this point that something unplanned and unexpected happened, which took the drama in a whole different direction. The clay mauri stone was accidently broken. This was not a careless act. Indeed, the teacher and researchers had previously noted that one of the children had placed it on the prayer table, an act that could be seen as a gesture of its significance and preciousness (see earlier photo). The stone got broken while a reliever teacher was in the class and some furniture was being moved around.

Elicia recalls what happened when she returned to the classroom and describes how she was able to use the event as a catalyst for creative work:

> The students were very worried. I didn't know how to handle this but [the event] became an inadvertent symbol! I went into role as Koro (from the story) and visited the class. The children had to explain to Koro how it happened. He suggested that they might be able to recreate/make their own mauri—take what they learned about the environment and put it into some clay—a new stone.

So, although not part of her original plan, Elicia responded to the real-life tension by inviting children to make clay pinch pots to symbolically recreate the lost mauri stone. This change of direction was only possible because Elicia was prepared to be flexible and responsive to events as they unfolded. If she had stuck rigidly to her plan she may have brushed the breaking of the stone aside. In the event, she endowed it with symbolic importance within the drama and turned it into another tension that drove the whole drama even more elegantly along the chosen theme of "creation".

Elicia really appreciated how, as with Banks's lost diary earlier in the unit, working from the dramatic tension added real purpose to the art activities:

> It wasn't like we're going to do clay birds and leaves because we are 'doing' the environment. There was a whole conceptual substance behind it. It stops being just an activity—it has purpose, meaning and understanding behind it.

Fig 7.10 *Clay pinch pots made by the children*

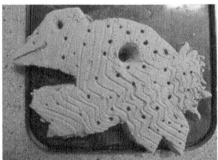

Fig 7.11 *A clay bird made by a child*

When the clay pots were completed, Elicia came back to the children in role as Koro and invited them (following Māori protocol) to imbue their work with mauri by breathing into it. As well as the pots, children created animals and other images representative of the life force, and Elicia noticed them "breathing mauri" into these too.

This conscious use of ritual can be seen as an instance of true integration, or perhaps incorporation of educational concerns at play in Elicia's classroom. Here, aspects of Māori spirituality, visual arts, social science, drama, environmental education and the values of the school's special character were incorporated in a very charged expression of the theme of creation. Children were invited to create objects of spiritual and personal significance and to reflect on the quality, not so much of the product, as of the act of creation in the very broadest sense of that word.

Following on from the clay making, Elicia encouraged the children to express the concept of mauri/life force through creative writing. Some of the poems produced by the children showed a striking use of imagery for a Year 3 class. Elicia commented:

Mauri is life and life giving like waves because it skims across the water like life skims across paintings and murals and water is needed by almost every creature on earth. Waves are crystal blue and shiny green like ferns. The blinding white foam goes under the water and pops up again like mauri across the years of history.

Fig 7.12 *Creative writing sample*

I believe their descriptive language was really elevated because they understood and believed the whole concept of life force—mauri. They understood it because they had lived the story—they were involved with it. They couldn't help but believe in it.

The unit continued with a return to the company identity and the original commission. In groups, the children created a blueprint suggesting how the land might be restored to respect what had gone before. A number of the children were inspired by information they discovered on the Internet about the Eden Project in the UK, and they proposed a domed structure containing a preserved example of the environment that Joseph Banks had seen.

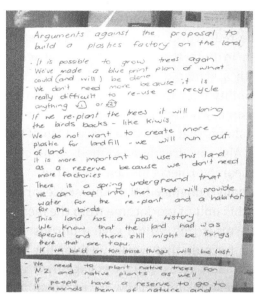

Fig 7.13 *Company representations to the council hearing*

A final lesson was framed as a council hearing whereby different groups' alternative development suggestions were formally presented. Elicia took the role of CEO of the plastics building company responsible for the original development plan and listened as, in groups, the children stood up to represent the client and shared their suggestions, backed up with evidence from the unit. The unit culminated with general out-of-role discussion on the issues raised, and children were invited to take their mauri stones and other clay creations home and keep them in a special place.

The children in Elicia's class took increased responsibility throughout this unit. Almost every task they undertook was framed as assisting or taking responsibility for something within the imagined world. This began with outlining their professional responsibilities within the company on the written reports, and continued with the reconstruction of Joseph Banks's diary. Stepping out of role as archaeologists, children were challenged to take responsibility for repairing the stone and returning the mauri to the whenua. Then, back in role as archaeologists, they were asked to speak up and take responsibility for a point of view or argument on an issue.

This was not a unit where children took on responsibility for decisions and actions in the real world, except of course that the broken mauri stone was broken in both the fictional and real worlds, so the ritual of repair was both a symbolic and actual redress. Children's sense of personal responsibility over their own learning also grew. Elicia kept a tally sheet of occasions when children took work home or brought things from home, and it shows that almost 70 percent (16 of the 23 children) did this at least once. Also, as already described, some children carried out quite extensive research projects in their own time.

Elicia is personally convinced that the sense of responsibility and wider purpose in this unit of work came from the fact that children were engaged in a high-status role, which gave a purpose to what they were doing. Elicia sees a formula that works well for her classroom: "It's like this: purpose plus adult roles equals engagement and intensity." The children's sense of responsibility grew in a gradual and organic way as the company was established and productive tensions were introduced. Elicia is clear that responsibility is not something that can simply be handed to children, but can only be grown into:

> It's really easy when teaching to think you've handed the power over but that can be a trap. There's a difference between saying 'Here you have my permission to take some power now' and the kids understanding the power they already have within them. The kind of thing I'm talking about here is something I've only noticed within a Mantle. It's not a sudden shift, or a gift from the teacher. It's a subtle process of growing into status. It is evidenced in their body language and their side conversations with you and with each other.

Elicia noticed a subtle change in the children's language register during this unit of work. In her teaching journal she described children developing a growing sense of what archaeologists do, and therefore what they are responsible for. She also described children deporting themselves as adults.

At the same time, Elicia found her own language register shifting. Elicia has always been a teacher who uses carefully crafted questions. In a systematic observation carried out in her classroom very early in the unit (27 April 2010), it was striking how often she expressed curiosity or interest (15 percent of recorded interactions) and how often she asked questions (15 percent) and co-constructed or negotiated with the children (9 percent). This questioning mode continued throughout the unit, and Elicia also felt that, as the unit went on, she increased her use of "genuine" questions (ones to which she does not have an answer). Elicia is clear that this kind of well-constructed genuine questioning is key to the promotion of children's responsibility and agency: "Your questions can either encourage or hinder agency. Questions can be an act of trust, or a bit of a pretence. This comes with practice."

Elicia also found herself exploring different models of classroom management. For example, she was keen to move away from the traditional "putting up hands" within the classroom since this is not the kind of thing that happens in an adult context. At first this was problematic, with children tending to parrot the agreed signal: "I'd like to add to that thinking", but Elicia says she has now evolved a new, more successful etiquette for listening and sharing within the classroom.

Outside of the research team, Elicia also found her practice informed by friends and associates. She recalls how Facebook conversations with her niece, a real-world archaeologist, provided important information about what archaeologists do, including the idea of reconstructing artefacts. Elicia also recalls an important conversation with a kuia (respected older woman) from her hometown that reminded her of some fundamentals about communication:

> She was referring to the fact that we depend on email and she gently reminded me of the power of kanohi ki te kanohi (face to face) ... She reminded me to think Māori. She reminded me: People make it real—reality exists in direct relationship.

Elicia is a highly relational teacher. However, these timely reminders from a respected figure outside of the school encouraged her to think about how she could enhance the "face-to-face" aspect of her teaching still further. The conversation fed into her decision to try using more teacher-in-role. Through role, Elicia was able to bring Joseph Banks, Koro and the plastics factory owner into the classroom for kanohi ki te kanohi interactions with the children.

Links to curriculum

Elicia's unit was very wide ranging in terms of curriculum coverage: in her own words, "We went everywhere—from asTTle to God!" Though not specifically linked to levels or achievement objectives, the unit incorporated drama (role taking, moments of ritual, mime), literacy (report writing, persuasive writing, creative writing, oral presentations), visual art (drawing, pastels and clay), languages (te reo Māori), social studies and history (the study of Joseph Banks), environmental education (discussions about land use) and ICT (creating business cards).

When encouraged to reflect on the pros and cons of the unit, one of the children in the class said that in his view there was not enough maths. Elicia acknowledged that greater opportunities for maths learning could have been incorporated (e.g., by including budgeting, measurement and estimation tasks related to the commission), as indeed she had done in the past. However, integration is not about covering every teaching area.

More micro-planned teaching could have occurred at certain stages of the Mantle of the Expert experience to deepen learning in a particular area, but that is not Elicia's preferred method of working. As she says:

> I've never had a problem to fly with the seat of my pants and always—no—sometimes—most times I have landed things. It's like I need to be on a knife edge for my brain to work best.

As suggested earlier, the true measure of value in this unit was not found at the level of achieving "learning intentions" or ticking off the strands or achievement objectives of particular curriculum areas, but in more holistic intentions related to key competencies and values. As O'Connor and Dunmill (2005) argue:

> The Arts provide a rich and meaningful context for the development of the five key competencies. Arts educators ... recognise the unique contribution the arts make to meaning making, to the development of arts thinking, of classrooms where teachers and students co-create art and new knowledge. (unpaged)

To put it in terms of *The New Zealand Curriculum* (Ministry of Education, 2007), this unit offered students learning experiences in a range of curriculum learning areas, including teaching and learning in and through the arts. Overall, the key emphasis was on values and key competencies. The unit also succeeded in bringing together Māori cultural values with the schoolwide Catholic character. All this was done within the innovative pedagogy of a Mantle of the Expert framework, so that students were positioned as competent co-creators of their own learning.

Conclusion

Elicia's work in this class attracted attention within the school and the wider region. The board of trustees visited the classroom and Elicia has continued to encourage others within the school to try using Mantle of the Expert in their teaching. She concedes that teaching in this way may not be for everyone, but describes a "coming home" feeling as she learns more about the pedagogy. This second attempt at teaching through Mantle of the Expert brought home to Elicia how complex the approach actually is: "Superficially, MOTE seems quite simple—use role and some conventions—but there's lots of layers."

Elicia has been thinking about how to maintain networking and professional development opportunities, as she wishes to continue to work in Mantle of the Expert:

> You can't learn it [Mantle of the Expert] from a book or from doing Mantle now and again. It's with sustained use that fine practice—that craft or art of managing the engagement through Mantle—gets better and better. That's what I witness in Luke [Abbott] and Dorothy [Heathcote]'s work and I'm in awe of it.

For Elicia, the answer lies in finding structures for face-to-face contact "Kanohi ki te kanohi—true for me too", with other teachers that will both support her and encourage her ongoing critique of her own practice and content.

A highly reflective, honest and self-critical person, Elicia realises that there is an ongoing dilemma of whose needs to meet in her teaching. She has her own needs or preferences as a nondirective, curious and trusting teacher, who keeps her planning to a minimum, flies "by the seat of her pants" and thinks best "on a knife edge". She acknowledges that, for her, the quality of learning in each learning area could be enhanced with more detailed planning, and this is something she aims to work on in future. Alongside her own teaching needs, she is also aware of the needs of a well-crafted Mantle of the Expert drama which involves awareness of phases, shifts in voice, crafted questions, carefully produced artefacts and subtle use of ritual, role and conventions.

At the same time, she is operating within a school that needs her to sustain its special character while also demonstrating achievement in an accountable way to outside agencies. A visit from the Education Review Office (ERO) has challenged her to think about how teachers using Mantle of the Expert can ensure that learning outputs stand up to outside monitoring and a call for more rigorous evidence of planning and achievement. Along with every other teacher in the current educational climate, Elicia is left navigating the relationship between learning, achievement and accountability. As Fraser (2012) and Lowe (2007) remind us, there are salient differences between learning and achievement even if, as a society, we often mistake the latter for the former:

> Learning is not the same as achievement ... Learning is a far deeper process manifested in a variety of ways that changes how we see and act in the world. (Fraser, 2012, p. 57)

In the face of these conflicting needs, and pressures, Elicia continues to strive to find ways of teaching that express her identity and her values; summed up in her phrase, "te mana te wehi me te ihi". As Palmer (1998) reminds us, identity and integrity are at the heart of all teaching:

> By identity and integrity I do not mean only our noble features, or the good deeds we do, or the brave faces we wear to conceal our confusions and complexities. Identity and integrity have as much to do with our shadows and limits, our wounds and fears, as with our strengths and potentials. (p. 13)

Palmer's words nicely encapsulate the spirit of Elicia's practice, both in terms of her reflection on her own teaching and the way in which she draws out and accommodates children in her class. Ultimately, Elicia is very clear where she wishes to place her focus: "What I need to work out is what the *children* need and go there!"

References

Ackroyd-Pilkington, J. (2001). Acting representation and role. *Research in Drama Education: The Journal of Applied Theatre and Performance, 6*(1), 9–22.

Balaisis, J. (2002). The challenge of teaching in role. *Applied Theatre Researcher*, *3*(3), 1–7.

Bowell, P., & Heap, B. (2002). *Planning process drama*. London: Fulton.

Edmiston, B. (2003). What's my position?: Role, frame and positioning when using process drama. *Research in Drama Education*, *8*(2), 221–229.

Fraser, D. (2012). The work and artistry of teaching. In C. McGee & D. Fraser (Eds.), *The professional practice of teaching* (4th ed., pp. 55–75). Melbourne: Cengage.

Heston, S. (n.d.). *The Dorothy Heathcote archive*. Manchester: Manchester Metropolitan University. Retrieved from http://www.did.stu.mmu.ac.uk/dha/hcheston.asp

Lowe, R. (2007). *The death of progressive education: How teachers lost control of the classroom*. London: Routledge.

Ministry of Education. (2007). *The New Zealand curriculum*. Wellington: Learning Media.

O'Connor, P., & Dunmill, M. (2005). *Key competencies and the arts in the New Zealand curriculum*. Retrieved from nzcurriculum.tki.org.nz/content/download/509/.../nzcmp-0805.doc

Palmer, P. J. (1998). *The courage to teach: Exploring the inner landscapes of a teacher's life*. San Francisco: Jossey-Bass.

Further resource

UK website for Mantle of the Expert: http://www.mantleoftheexpert.com

CHAPTER EIGHT

When Tragedy Strikes: School Community Renewal Through Arts Inquiry

Barbara Whyte with Nikki Keys

Introduction

An arson attack on Welcome Bay School burnt two classrooms to the ground, and the unit described in this chapter arose literally from the ashes. The fire devastated the school community and emotionally traumatised staff and children, who lost valuable resources. It also created pressure, as classes, children and teaching spaces were shuffled about until relocatable classrooms were eventually installed onsite. The fire occurred when a relatively new leadership team at the school was in the process of re-visioning the school, developing the concept of "The Welcome Bay School Learner" (WBS Learner) and considering the questions: "Who are we as a community?" "Who are our learners?" "What are our learners' needs?" Within the context of the re-visioning process the fire provided the impetus for the school community to contemplate a further question: "Where to now?"

The overwhelming response to that question from the children was:

> We need to work on the environment so that other people want to be here and be proud of it too. If it's a great place to be in, then others won't damage it.

A decision was made to involve the whole school in an arts inquiry as a means of deciding on what was needed to improve the school environment. The inquiry was to be a negotiation between children and staff, and the drive for action would come from the ideas generated by the children. To gather ideas and inspiration, the entire school piled into buses for a day to explore various public art and landscapes in Tauranga and the wider Bay of Plenty area as far as Katikati. The focus question for the trip was, "What makes an inviting environment?" Nikki reported:

> The children were abuzz with ideas when all the buses converged for a lunch break. The children excitedly compared the mosaic stonework on footpaths in the inner city and suburbs; identified what had motivated them at the range of schools visited; recognised the value of sensory and sound gardens; debated the merits of Katikati's town murals and those in Greerton Village; and argued about the meanings and merits of the various sculptural art forms seen in and about Tauranga (as well as those they were currently viewing over lunch at Te Puna Quarry Park, which houses a variety of artists' work). I was blown away by the quality of their observations and critique.

The big idea

On returning to school, each classroom's discussion enabled teachers to gain an insight into children's preferences from what had been viewed, and what might be worthwhile implementing in the school. It was the children's deliberations that reinforced for staff that there were clear links with the previously established attributes of the WBS Learner. In particular, staff noticed the key attribute of "standing proud" being translated by the children into the big idea of "being proud of your environment". Staff detected that children interpreted that idea as meaning two things:

- They could come up with ideas of artworks that would look attractive in the school and make them proud.
- Children were able to come up with their own ideas about how to make the school environment look attractive.

Those ideas could be actioned, and that in itself was rewarding. It was clear that the need to renew the school environment provided an authentic context that was both motivating and purposeful for the children.

From their classroom discussions, each class negotiated and decided on a preferred concept for enhancing an area of the school environment. This was followed by a plan of action outlining costs and materials, and the ways they intended to develop their concept, which the classes presented to the principal as a formally written document. Nikki noted the thoroughness of the in-class processing, and the resulting detail required considerable use of different literacy and mathematics skills. It also meant that, generally, each concept plan of action was approved with little need for revision.

The hook

The fire provided the catalyst for the children to consider how to rebuild and visually enhance their school environment. However, the hook for the children was the agentic opportunity to turn dreams into reality via a whole-school project. With concept plans approved, the next step was to put them into action. A dedicated "Art Week" was decided on by staff and student leaders as a way of providing a concentrated period of time when the entire school would work together to bring their separate class plans to fruition. It was the prospect and promise of the Art Week that enticed the children to engage in the enhancement project for the school environment.

Organising for learning

The Art Week proved to be highly motivating in two ways. The initial motivation of in-class projects led by the children became integrated units leading up to the Art Week, which entailed research and information gathering. One example is the sensory garden and the breadth of the task involved for the class that instigated this topic. A detailed plan of visual, fragrant and touchable plantings, plus complementary play structures, was approved by the principal. However, the children still needed to find out the types of plants that fitted the above categories, such as those that are fragrant, visually appealing, edible, audible (emit sound when touched) and/or tactile. They also needed to research the features of these plants, such as:

- flowers, foliage, size when mature, what fragrance (or sound) is released
- what plants might be hardy enough to survive school playground conditions

- where such plants could be acquired
- how the soil needed to be prepared and cultivated before planting
- what ongoing plant care was required after planting
- exact measurements of the allocated space for the sensory garden
- how to integrate the plants within a playground "trail" activity so that plants that release a fragrance when crushed, or that feel soft or textured when landed upon, are placed in appropriate sequences with play structures
- what structures would be inviting, child-friendly and safe, yet motivating for children to play there
- who could provide recycled materials to construct the structures
- who could help construct the structures
- how to meet the budget constraints
- the sequence of events and a timeline to ensure the sensory garden became a reality during the Art Week time frame.

The second motivation came from children working as apprentices alongside adult artists who were willing to focus on environmental art. It was an early idea to tap into the expertise of artists from the wider community, and interest was generated through the school making contact with garden artists and with Creative Tauranga, an organisation promoting the arts in Tauranga. As a result, artists such as painters and sculptors, along with environmental artists, offered their skills and became directly involved with the various classroom-initiated projects. The artists' involvement created a two-fold approach: groups of children worked with the artists to learn art processes, and the artists facilitated the creative process by enabling the children to take their negotiated classroom designs and concept plans through to final products. The art works were created in a variety of forms and dimensions, and some required considerable construction.

In Nikki's view, the beauty of having diverse aspects to the projects provided an opportunity for children with identified talents to work alongside others in the school with similar skills, rather than just their usual class peers. So, children who were talented in visual art were invited to work alongside visual artists; those with talents in construction were invited to work with wood or concrete and mesh, to build sculptures and structures alongside garden and environment artists; and those with an interest and talent in Māori art were invited to create Māori-themed two- and three-dimensional art works alongside a Māori artist. Burnaford, Aprill and Weiss (2001) describe a project (CAPE) that similarly brought professional artists and schools together to bridge community–school divides and foster learning for students and teachers. In this project, artists and teachers co-planned and integrated arts learning into other academic disciplines to create meaningful curriculum. Integration beyond the arts was also a feature of the school's restoration project. The ways in which other learning areas were incorporated are outlined below.

Deepening the learning

During Art Week the classrooms and playground areas became a hive of activity. There were visual artists working with groups of children to create painted corrugated-iron story panels, wood-and-bamboo story totem poles, huge mosaic panels representing WBS Learner attributes and large-scale murals. There were environmental artists and children helping to construct and plant a corrugated iron palm tree, creating and installing mosaic garden features in amongst plantings and sculpting concrete creatures such as a whale. There were teachers working alongside children, and artists preparing sites by digging out old plants, digging over new plant beds, mixing concrete, manoeuvring child-decorated posts and structures into place and using tools to cut sheets of tin for corrugated iron murals. There were also groups of children regularly working at an artist's personal studio creating huge thrones.

The caretaker was involved, supervising the bigger plant-moving and removing ventures, helping to get heavy equipment to where it was needed and ensuring child safety was paramount.

Children had to self-manage (a key competency in the curriculum) over the week, because the usual routines and timetables were disrupted. As a result they had to work out their own appropriate times for nutrition and rest and negotiate these with teachers. Nikki got used to rain-checks from the children: "Time for lunch" was often met with "No … can't stop right now … later." She adds that all week there was a "Huge sense of team.

Fig 8.1 *Principal and caretaker position a learning throne*

It was a bit like the TV *Garden Makeover* programme—everyone doing their little bit for the good of the whole." Such collaboration, connection-making, participating and contributing helps to foster the sense of belonging advocated by the curriculum (Ministry of Education, 2007).

The Art Week was clearly integrated curriculum. Enviro-Schools, visual arts, social sciences and technology were incorporated and the school's vision of the WBS Learner attributes (stand proud, show courage, ask questions, seek adventure and have a heart), were woven throughout the children's concepts, designs and decorative patterning. Following are a number of examples:

- Having particularly enjoyed the inner-city footpath mosaics seen on the bus trip, a Years 5/6 class decided to display the five attributes in this mode and invited a school parent from the Tauranga Mosaic Group to show them the process of creating mosaics. Large mosaic representations of the five attributes were created by the class as a school footpath. The parent continued to work alongside the class for several weeks, giving advice and ideas for the project.

- Five "Thrones of Learning and Creativity" were designed to represent the five WBS Learner attributes. The children who worked on the thrones were the student leaders, who were selected for this special task because it reflected the next visual representation or chapter of the WBS Learner and the school. The thrones were created at a local artist's studio and the student leaders shuttled back and forth each day between the studio and the school. The completed thrones were transported triumphantly to the school and set in place around a covered courtyard with appropriate pomp and ceremony.

Fig 8.2 *School community landscaping*

Fig 8.3 *Thrones of Learning and Creativity*

- Different classes contributed to collaborative murals that depicted school learning stories. Classroom teachers led the mural making, assisted by artists invited to help guide the process. The resulting murals reflected the children's story-telling, decision making, co-operation, co-construction and mounting of final products.
- All gardens within the school grounds were relandscaped. Each area of the school with a garden was assigned to children to redesign. Children negotiated with others to decide on the most appropriate

space for their project. Some also chose to develop new raised-bed vegetable gardens in sunny spots within the playground. Expertise from the teacher leading Enviro-Schools at WBS fostered the garden development, with children researching the best way to position, prepare, plant and maintain their different gardens. This Art Week landscaping eventually became an ongoing project, with children opting to become part of the garden group on a long-term basis.

- "100 trees" was an orchard planted during Art Week, designed with the long-term objective of providing a resource the community could access in the future. Another school project, Healthy Eating–Healthy Action (HEHA, developed earlier out of an Enviro-Schools contract), provided funding for the purchase of the fruit trees, and the children bargained and negotiated with the HEHA committee over a good price for the trees.

- Gardens that stimulate the senses (mentioned earlier) became a collaborative syndicate project. One class investigated the sorts of plants that give off aromas and can be eaten, and how to cultivate them. This motivated their syndicate to take the concept further and to collaborate in the creation of a more extensive sensory garden. Each class in the syndicate came up with a concept for a section of the sensory garden, then negotiated across the syndicate on how to combine the individual designs into one cohesive sensory garden enterprise.

- The children expressed the need to have something to interact with in the new landscaped environment. The concept of the sound garden seen and heard at Te Puna Quarry Park readily translated to a WBS recycled sound garden designed and constructed by a group of children. During Art Week they made brightly patterned free-standing xylophones with timber off-cuts gathered from the community. They also formed percussion instruments from donated pot lids, and created wind-chimes out of recycled bamboo segments retrieved from the school grounds, painting these with personal story designs. The children took durability, access and aesthetics into consideration when planning and constructing such items, which were designed to be used.

The integrated curriculum events described above show how the arts can be a source of insight and practice in quality education. Wilson (2008) argues for children's art experiences to be considered as collaboration, because in taking this stance children are positioned as competent co-creators of learning and co-constructors of meaning. Eisner (2008) argues for the practical implications of the arts in real-life situations, and it is clear that Art Week stimulated pragmatic activities imbued with essential curriculum content.

Fig 8.4 *Constructing a musical instrument for a sound garden*

Nikki noted that Art Week started enthusiastically enough but really gained momentum when the school community realised and accepted the extent of the project. As the week progressed the community saw what was happening and sensed the zeal and interest of the children. Word quickly got around that the school welcomed involvement, and suddenly extra artists offered to contribute their time. People from the local community also arrived; some revealed artistic talents unknown until the project, while others provided essential construction skills such as carpentry and concrete-mixing. From Nikki's perspective, observable by-products from this community involvement were parent and caregiver sharing of knowledge, teamwork and relationship forming with the school. She noted that:

> There were parents sitting comfortably in the staffroom, feeling a part of the school, who had not previously had much contact—a sense of 'all in together'. I believe they saw the project as an opportunity to work alongside their children and learn together.

Fig 8.5 *Parent and staff member collaborate on art works*

As children worked with real artists they gained insight that there are people in the community who make artworks as a job and that in the future this might be a career for some of them. The student leaders working in a local artist's studio learnt that artists are creative people who effectively work with a range of media, but when involved in a project with others, need to self-manage, meet deadlines, relate to others and communicate effectively (see the key competencies of *The New Zealand Curriculum* (Ministry of Education, 2007)), just as with any other job. The Art Week activities highlighted the importance of being in a community and the roles and responsibilities associated with being part of a group. Fraser (2012) notes that incorporating such outside experts helps to build vibrant school programmes.

Fig 8.6 *Children "plant" a corrugated iron tree*

A real bonus of the project was the interest and contribution generated by the Māori community. There were offerings of expertise in fields such as landscaping, concrete-mixing, building, Māori arts and crafts (tukutuku, whakairo and kōwhaiwhai design), and organisational skills. Acknowledging the large proportion of Māori students (54 percent) in the school, Nikki was keen to attract an artist to capture the cultural ideas and perspectives of Māori students. Art Week saw a Māori community member volunteer to lead some art activities. This artist impressed staff with the ease with which he established and maintained rapport with the group of boys who chose to work with him. Staff noted that by positioning the boys as competent co-constructors of their learning, they responded extremely positively to his leadership. The artist impulsively provided kai one lunchtime for this group, and Nikki said:

> This drew out an in-depth discussion of their conceptualisations of Māori art—over fish and chips! The boys stuck to him like glue for the week. They really focused on their tasks and strived to achieve high-quality products.

The artist facilitated the boys' sense of ownership and achievement and was obviously an effective role model. The boys later expressed pride in the carvings and paintings they produced, some of which featured on the outside wall of one of the buildings leading into the school. Bishop and Berryman (2006) note in their Effective Teaching Profile that kotahitanga (unity) and culturally appropriate contexts facilitate learning for Māori students.

Fig 8.7 *Māori art elements in wall paintings*

Links to curriculum

An integrated curriculum approach to learning (Beane, 1997; Brough, 2008; Dowden, 2007; Fraser, 2000) was included in all the classrooms.

The arts
Visual arts across all four arts strands (Understanding in Context, Practical Knowledge, Developing Ideas and Communicating & Interpreting) were demonstrated in the following ways:
- viewing the art and landscape ideas created by others on the bus trip
- exploration of different construction and decorative materials that would be robust in a school playground

- creating visual concepts illustrative of events and personal stories important to the children in the school, alongside real artists
- sharing and communicating these ideas in their final landscape art products.

One of the children acknowledged the value of having a week-long concentrated arts focus:

... when you concentrate on the others [other curriculum areas] it takes you away from creativity—your brain is like mixed up with other things—but an art week lets us have creativity in the brain for a whole week. (Petra)

Fig 8.8 *A girl completes part of a mural*

English

Speaking, writing and presenting: oral literacy—communicating with others at levels appropriate to the age of children; for example:

- juniors—more structured direction and modelling from teachers
- middle school—negotiation with teacher, driven by class ideas
- seniors—more individual leadership, with teacher facilitation.

Science

Living world (life processes of plants and trees; as prepared, planted and maintained in the school gardens; the human senses; the sensory garden, the sound garden—how key elements of these gardens linked to the senses). An interesting question from the children once they started on the Art Week activities, and which prompted further investigation, was: "What happens to the creatures already in the environment, when a new environment is created and old areas are dismantled and redesigned?"

Mathematics and statistics

Number and algebra: patterns and relationships were identified when gardens and art works were being planned and implemented. One child pinpointed her curriculum understanding of the orchard and garden projects within a variety of mathematical concepts:

You're doing science learning about the plants and how to grow them and all that, but you're kind of doing maths because you've got to organise how much fruit to hand out to each person. Sort of like the times tables. You have to think about how many rows you have to plant, and lay out the plan and plant the seeds—so there's geometry—and then work out how much water to give each plant—and that's measurement. (Bethany)

Another child linked environmental concepts with number strategies:

If we took all the things [school waste] for 1 month to our rugby field and worked it out for 12 [months] it'd be about 30 stories high. But if we composted and re-cycled we could halve that—and that would be fractions—and if we were very good at it, we could halve that again—and that would be more fractions. (McKenzie)

Health

(i)   Relationships with other people; interpersonal skills—required by the children when working collaboratively within the school, with each other and with the wider community as they went through the process of creating physical products to enhance the school environment.

(ii) Healthy communities and environment: community resources— the school community and school can work co-operatively to create an environment that all can use and for which they have a shared sense of ownership and guardianship. One child articulated her understanding of this strand in the attitudes and values she perceived from the "100 trees" orchard project:

Planting an orchard in the school may be unusual, but it's good for everyone— just giving away fruit and stuff. It's good for the health of the kids like those at school with no lunch and visitors coming to the school who might be hungry. (Stephanie)

Technology

(i)   Technological practice: planning for practice—developing concept plans; brief and outcome development (identifying process to product costing, resourcing, structuring design, use of materials, budgeting, logistics, organisation, project management and meeting deadlines).

(ii) Technological knowledge: understanding and planning for robustness, material appropriateness for the designs and using processes that fulfil those requirements (e.g., concrete-mixing and carpentry).

Key competencies

One of the exciting aspects of the Art Week project for Nikki was witnessing children working overtly with the key competencies. She noticed children thinking about changes to be made to the school environment and coming up with new ideas; using language, symbols and text to express, share and communicate these ideas with others and solve problems in a wide range of situations; self-managing as the Art Week days became less structured and usual classroom routines and timetables dissipated; relating to others by being flexible and adaptable to the ideas of others, collaborating, communicating with peers and adults, having a voice and building relationships with others they may not normally work with; and participating and contributing with school peers and community towards a mutual goal, with everyone having a part to play in both the process and the product.

Conclusion

This school community project resulted in a large amount of learning and understanding. The first aspect Nikki commented on concerned the enormous task of restoring the school environment after the devastation of the fire. The practicalities of doing this in a democratic way were, in her view, "huge". She noted:

> Organising a whole-school inquiry is a massive undertaking—quite different to organising an inquiry for children in one classroom. The aim is the same, but the practical organisation for giving 200 children the same lens to view art and have a voice about what they viewed—and then ensure their ideas could become a reality—was huge! The commitment from staff and children was impressive. The excitement from staff was infectious. They set their expectations very high, and even though the logistics were a headache, in the end, the pain was worth it!

A positive outcome of rallying together a whole-school inquiry has been the noticeable decline in damage on the weekends to the school environment since the Art Week. The children are very proud of the artworks and landscaping and the community has become quite protective of the school. Following the Art Week, the most positive aspect for the children is that they are able to continue working with local artists to create further "chapters" of art under the umbrella of the WBS Learner concept and within the story of the restoration of the school and its environment. Nikki noted:

> Only a week was allowed for—the core was established then—but the project continues. Everyone wants to see the whole thing finished, but now realise it is ongoing and that it is with us for many more years to come.

Interestingly, this ongoing nature of the events has contributed to increased community involvement with the school. For example, following involvement in the Art Week, a dad in the school organised and set up regular "Blokes' Breakfasts" at the school. This gave caregivers whose jobs precluded them from being involved in the school during the working day an opportunity to connect with and show their interest in the school. Similarly, a caregiver took the initiative to create, publish and distribute a local Whānau Newsletter that focused on school and community events. The HEHA committee (mentioned earlier) looked for further ways to raise funds to help add and maintain sensory plants to the school grounds, and provided support and assistance for those children wanting to be part of a continuing garden group. And a caregiver, pleased with the welcome she received from the school during the Art Week, spontaneously cooked and shared special food from her ethnic group with staff during one of her important cultural celebrations.

The arts inquiry demonstrated the power of children working together towards a common goal, and the Art Week activities nurtured the notion that "we are in this together as community". The sense of community strengthened by the collaborative Art Week project aligns with McMillan's (1996) definition of community as:

> A spirit of belonging together, a feeling that there is an authority structure that can be trusted, an awareness that trade, and mutual benefit come from being together, and a spirit that comes from shared experiences that are preserved as art. (p. 315)

The healing, restoration and renewal achieved by recreating and transforming the environment together has reinforced a sense of community for everyone involved and underlined the feeling that guardianship of the school surroundings is shared among children, teachers and the community.

References

Beane, J. (1997). *Curriculum integration: Designing the core of democratic education.* New York: Teachers College Press.

Bishop, R., & Berryman, M. (2006). *Culture speaks: Cultural relationships and classroom learning.* Wellington: Huia.

Brough, C. (2008). Student-centred curriculum integration and the New Zealand curriculum. *set: Research Information for Teachers, 2,* 16–21.

Burnaford, G., Aprill, A., & Weiss, C. (2001). *Renaissance in the classroom: Arts integration and meaningful learning.* Mahwah, NJ: Lawrence Erlbaum Associates.

Dowden, T. (2007). Relevant, challenging, integrative and exploratory curriculum design: Perspectives from theory and practice for middle level schooling in Australia. *Australian Educational Researcher, 34*(2), 51–71.

Eisner, E. (2008, March). *What education can learn from the arts.* Lowenfeld lecture, presented at the NAEA national convention, New Orleans, Louisiana.

Fraser, D. (2000). Curriculum integration: What it is and is not. *set: Research Information for Teachers, 3,* 34–37.

Fraser, D. (2012). Developing classroom culture: Creating a climate for learning. In C. McGee & D. Fraser (Eds.), *The professional practice of teaching* (4th ed., pp. 1–20), Melbourne, VIC: Cengage.

McMillan, D. (1996). Sense of community. *Journal of Community Psychology, 24*(4), 315–325.

Ministry of Education. (2007). *The New Zealand curriculum.* Wellington: Learning Media.

Wilson, B. (2008, August). *The end of child art and the emergence of adult/kid collaborative conjunctions in three pedagogical sites.* Keynote address to the 32nd International Society for Education through Art world congress, Osaka, Japan.

CHAPTER NINE

Tsunami: Social Action in the Real World

Deborah Fraser with Penny Deane

Introduction

At 7 am on 29 September 2009 an earthquake of magnitude 8.2 triggered a tsunami, which hit Samoa. The worst-affected areas were in the north, including devastation to the villages of Salea'aumua, Saleapaga and Satitoa on the island of Upolu. Satitoa school was completely destroyed and other schools were so badly water damaged that they were structurally unsafe. Events like this invariably touch New Zealanders deeply given the numbers of kiwis of Samoan descent and the connections New Zealand has culturally and historically with the South Pacific.

As with most disasters, after the initial donations the aid started to dry up. Clean-up and rebuilding tended to focus on the tourist spots, but the destruction of homes, schools and communities was basically neglected. Three months later in the non-tourist areas it still looked like a scene of devastation. Added to this were heavy tropical rains making transport and rebuilding difficult. The following is a summary of how one Year 3 class responded to the tragedy, and how the children with their teacher learnt that they can help others even in the most difficult circumstances.

The big idea

With curriculum integration, inquiry usually begins with a central issue of concern that has real personal and social significance for children (Beane, 1997, 2005). In this case, the issue included social concerns, consciousness raising and a wide range of learning across the curriculum. These are the goals of curriculum integration and align with the aims of *The New Zealand Curriculum* (Ministry of Education, 2007).

Fig 9.1 *Wreckage from the tsunami*

The hook

At Omanu School in the Bay of Plenty, a Year 3 girl returned to school after the holidays and shared with her teacher stories of the devastation she had witnessed first hand in Samoa when the tsunami struck. She had been on holiday in Samoa at the time with her mother and Samoan-born grandfather. They did what they could to support the most affected areas, collecting money from hotel guests and taking supplies to the worst-hit villages. Once back in New Zealand, her mother and teacher discussed ways in which they could sustain a support effort to help rebuild lives in Samoa. The discussion grew to include the class, with the natural catalyst coming from the child's personal experience and her family's concern about the after-effects of the disaster. Media coverage also heightened awareness for this class of Year 3 children.

Organising for learning

The class, in negotiation with their teacher and the child's mother, decided to focus their support efforts on Satitoa School. The five-room school had been completely destroyed; all that remained was the concrete pad on which the school had once stood. Focusing on the school enabled the children to empathise and connect, drawing on their own experience as school children. However, research was required to piece together what was needed as the teacher realised that the differences between the two countries could result in offering irrelevant or inappropriate goods and materials. The children's need to study the geography, culture and customs of Samoa therefore had a real and urgent purpose. The more they knew, the more likely they were to be able to make a difference.

Fig 9.2 *A boat swept inland*

In curriculum integration, an issue or problem is often the catalyst for a unit, and this is followed by children identifying their prior knowledge and then investigating what they need to know. Children's questions helped to frame their investigation, and these multiplied as they discovered more about Satitoa. The questions included:

- What do they need right now?
- What have they lost?
- What might they need in a few weeks' time?
- What sorts of food are best to gather?
- What clothing do they wear?
- How can we make sure that what we send finds the children that need what we have collected?
- How are the children feeling?
- Would they like some of my toys?
- What games do they play?

Initial thoughts were to get a container and fill it with things that might be useful. However, they soon learnt that there was much more to it than that.

Deepening the learning

The children began to list the items required for re-stocking a school. These included school bags, paper, pencils, books, desks and chairs, shelving units, pinboards, whiteboards, blackboards, fans and filing cabinets. However, they soon discovered that school life could not be separated from home and community life. Their research, with the skilful guidance of their teacher, enabled them to add items that were required by the Samoan school children's families and community. As more information about the effects of the tsunami was gathered, they realised the children and their families needed (among other things) clothing for all ages, basic survival and cooking equipment, tools, storage containers for food and water, recreational equipment, buckets, mosquito nets, rakes, brooms and toiletries.

The class soon realised that to attempt to meet such a vast array of needs they needed to ask for help from the broader local community. Through a series of communications, including emails, faxes, letters, posters and asking around, the class rallied the support of 16 local schools and kindergartens and a large number of businesses.

Fig 9.3 *Children's posters and notices for the collection campaign*

Over a 6-week period the children successfully gathered the teaching and learning materials, games, physical education equipment, storage and shelving, pinboards, clocks, blackboards, stationery, art gear, cleaning and basic maintenance equipment needed to reopen Satitoa School. Every child from the school was sent a new school bag with the stationery required for a year's education. In addition, one of the most touching things the New Zealand children decided to do was to send each child at Satitoa a care box. Discussion and debate ensued about what should go in the boxes. They decided that the items had to be useful and environmentally appropriate. They thought about what would be gender neutral as they did not know whether their care box would be received by a girl or a boy. They then listed and debated what might be welcomed by children in Satitoa. As these care boxes would go to individual children, they added a personal touch in terms of a handwritten letter, introducing themselves and saying how they were thinking of the children of Satitoa. The care boxes contained items such a marbles, skipping ropes, puppets, toiletries, soap, toothbrushes, toothpaste, comics, sunglasses and hats.

As news of the classroom's aid event spread, many businesses came on board, donating a range of goods. A parent donated an old rusty shipping container in which the class could house and transport the donated goods. A trucking company then offered to paint and sign-write the container to spruce it up. Pacific Blue Airlines donated three air tickets so that the

169

teacher, mother and grandfather (mentioned at the outset) could collect the container when it docked. They also worked with the Samoan Ministry of Education, the local council of matai and disaster relief co-ordinators to ensure that cultural protocols were observed and goods were delivered safely to the new school site.

Fig 9.4 *Boys with a care box they put together for a child in Satitoa*

Fig 9.5 *The donated and decorated shipping container*

Links to curriculum

Clearly, an extensive project like this draws on a range of curriculum subject areas. These are outlined briefly below and examples of the children's learning are given.

Mathematics

Mathematics links included: measurement of blackboards and pinboards; capacity (How many banana boxes fit in a shipping container?); time (international time differences, shipping dates and passages); statistics (graphing to keep track of ideas and results); numeracy (keeping track of purchases and donations; counting in multiples, such as 20 tennis balls per bag); money and problem solving (How many pairs of scissors does a class need? A school need? What is the total cost, and can it be afforded?).

Technology

Technology links included: emails, faxes, Internet searches, and camera and video use for record keeping.

The Arts

Arts links included: examining the dance, music and visual art of Samoa.

Reading and Writing

Reading and writing links included: making posters to advertise fund raising; emails and faxes to and from local schools and businesses; emails from the Samoan Ministry of Education; letters to children in Satitoa; writing notes home (and reminders); scripting speeches.

Oral Language

Oral language links included: hosting guests and sharing learning; negotiating a bargain with various businesses; preparing thank-you speeches; preparing questions for visiting experts (e.g., Samoan family members, workers at Bunnings, when working with other adults on joint projects).

Social Studies

Social Studies links included: understanding that people have social, cultural and economic roles, rights and responsibilities; understanding how time and change affect people's lives; understanding how places influence people and people influence places.

Key competencies

All the key competencies were evident within this integrated unit, but in particular the learning the children undertook highlighted relating to others, and participating and contributing. In terms of the former, they were involved in negotiating the aid project with classmates, their teacher, the wider school, other schools, homes and businesses. They were actively involved in problem solving, investigating and being creative. The children ran some hard bargains with building companies and sought the best prices. However, they soon learnt that a number of places would donate materials once they knew what the purpose was.

In terms of participating and contributing, they experienced first hand what it means to be part of a community project, what it means to contribute beyond the needs of oneself and one's family, and what it means to support people in another country. Such experiences underline the moral challenge in education: teachers do not just teach subjects. Whether it is overt or not, everything that is taught is value-laden and values underpin what it means to be educated. *The New Zealand Curriculum* (Ministry of Education, 2007) was reflected in the project, with its values emphasis on:

- inquiry into what was needed in Satitoa
- diversity in terms of Samoan culture
- equity with regard to supporting others in times of need
- sustainability in terms of ongoing community, village and school life
- respect for local Samoan protocols
- contribution to "the common good".

Brough notes that during curriculum integration, values and key competencies "are not add-ons taught through isolated lessons; rather, they are interwoven throughout" (2008, p. 13). For teachers wanting to emulate a rich inquiry such as this one, the first step is to take notice of the events that have real significance for their children and their families. These are the events that concern them and have keen relevance for their lives. Inviting questions, devising plans, negotiating investigations, refining ideas and contacting community members all stem from a need-to know-basis: they are not driven by assessment requirements or a completely pre-planned unit of work.

Conclusion

This chapter provides a case study of curriculum integration, whereby a teacher and her class collaboratively investigated the needs of a Samoan school devastated by a tsunami. The project included a variety of community support and involvement. The children drew upon a range of curriculum areas and key competencies within the authentic context of the extensive aid project. In effect, this integrated project reflects the curriculum goal of children as "active seekers, users and creators of knowledge" (Ministry of Education, 2007, p. 8). It also provides an example of promoting children's agency through socially responsive activism.

Proponents of national standards in numeracy and literacy have much to consider here. Not only were numeracy and literacy evident in the children's learning, but there was also a clear, relevant and important purpose for working with number and words. The work the children undertook was far beyond the fulfilment of an assessment task or the completion of a set class activity. The children were involved in negotiations and decisions that had implications for the quality of life of others, and they showed the grit and compassion to follow the project through. Barker (2012) reminds us that we must not steal the learning from our students. If we focus too narrowly on certain targets and assessments, we miss the deeper goals that emerge during an integrated project of this nature. Even children as young as Year 3 can be fully involved in an aid project, which expands their sense of responsibility and contribution and enables them to appreciate their capacity to make a difference. As Beane asserts, children deserve a curriculum that takes them seriously as agents of social change:

> We should ask that the curriculum challenge our young people to imagine a
> better world and try out ways of making it so. We should ask that it bring them

justice and equity, that it help them to overcome the narrow prejudices still so evident in our society. (2005, p. 136)

The work the class undertook was highly collaborative, socially mediated and negotiated. The groundswell of support they engendered from the wider community says much about the worth of the cause. Noteworthy is the fact that this was not a one-off event but has created an enduring relationship between Omanu and Satitoa. The teacher, her colleagues and members of the school community have visited the Samoan school several times in the ensuing years, establishing a bond between the schools that is expected to be ongoing. This example of curriculum integration shows that limitations are few and possibilities are many. And through the process, both teacher and children learn it is not too bold to imagine, and create, a better world.

Acknowledgements

This chapter is a revised version of the article: D. Fraser & P. Deane. (2010). Making a difference: Agents of change through curriculum integration. *set: Research Information for Teachers*, *3*, 10–14 (reprinted with permission).

References

Barker, M. (2012). How do people learn?: Understanding the learning process. In C. McGee & D. Fraser (Eds.), *The professional practice of teaching* (4th ed., pp. 21–54). Melbourne, VIC: Cengage.

Beane, J. (1997). *Curriculum integration: Designing the core of democratic education*. New York, NY: Teachers College Press.

Beane, J. (2005). *A reason to teach: Creating classrooms of dignity and hope*. Portsmouth, NH: Heinemann.

Brough, C. (2008). Student-centred curriculum integration in action: "I was wondering if you could tell me how much one meat patty and one sausage costs?" *set: Research Information for Teachers*, *3*, 9–14.

Ministry of Education. (2007). *The New Zealand curriculum*. Wellington: Learning Media.

CHAPTER TEN

Picture the Writing

Deborah Fraser with Gay Gilbert

Introduction

This chapter highlights how teachers can connect poetic writing with visual art in ways that honour both disciplines and deepen the learning. In contrast to the other chapters in this book, the unit described here draws on just two subject areas. There is merit in limiting the scope like this, as the following discussion reveals. The pedagogy described here is based on Gay Gilbert's many years of teaching and her work in leading whole-school development in literacy and the arts. Gay is the deputy principal of a large, urban, multicultural school. She has an abiding passion for both the arts and literacy. She strongly believes in writing that stems from children's interests and views of the world, and in the value of deepening aesthetic perception when writing is integrated with visual art.

Gay uses writing and art to stimulate the child's unique response to his or her world. She deliberately uses these to help children notice the richness of their world and capture it in an intensely focused and personal way. To reinforce the value of this, she makes comments to children such as, "You will never be this age again, so that's why you want to capture this now and the way you feel." The gems children write are also illustrated by them in ways that honour visual expression. As this chapter will show, the art work is much more than mere decoration for the all-powerful text. If visual art is used alongside literacy it is often relegated to the status of decorative border or quick drawing, rather than the starting point of observation. In addition, the primacy of the writing means that the visual art is the last aspect considered and the first to go if a child is short on time. Too often such art work is perceived by teachers as recreational "rather than as providing a significant medium for children to explore and communicate their imaginations and creative mental capacities" (Wright, 2010, p. 177).

When it comes to expressive writing, Gay promotes the view that every child is an author and the teacher's job is to bring forth the child's original voice. For years Gay has motivated and taught children to create their own anthologies of what she terms "exciting writing". These contain a variety of written pieces by children that are carefully constructed and polished. Through this they discover their writer's voice. The writing is also illustrated in ways that transcend the decorative and adds aesthetic value as visual art. Many of the children Gay has taught have kept their books as real treasures. Some have passed these on to their own children, creating a legacy of personal writing and illustrations that are intergenerationally cherished. This clearly indicates the value children (and adults) place on this work.

Gay's passion for this form of integration is part and parcel of her creative approach to pedagogy. She also acknowledges the influence of mentors such as Stan Boyle and the legacy of Elwyn Richardson (1972, 2003, 2012). Richardson was instrumental in creating the "Oruaiti experiment" (as it came to be called) in the far north of New Zealand, developing a school that focused strongly on science and the arts. His work with children at that school was later published in his seminal book, *In the Early World* (Richardson, 1972), in which he shares his child-centred approach to education. He argued that education should foster children's intense interests and tap their emotional energies. Much of his pedagogy reflected integration of curriculum, with the initial impetus coming from an environmental source. Thus, the children often worked outdoors, carefully observing flora and fauna, taking notes and making observational drawings. They would also dig clay for pottery and build their own kilns. The skills of art making were learned alongside the skills of science, and the writing children developed emerged from their absorption in creative and scientific experiences. Richardson realised that children's intense experiences were the doorway to knowledge.

In a similar vein, Sylvia Ashton-Warner advocated key vocabulary, which she believed educated children from the inside rather than imposing meaning from the outside (Jones & Middleton, 2009). For example, the key vocabulary was drawn from words children offered that had direct meaning and emotional impact, based on their actual experiences and deep-seated feelings. The roots of her work are evident in what is now termed the "language experience" approach, which is widely used in New Zealand schools.

A further influential figure for Gay is Gail Loane (2010), who offers professional development for teachers on enriching and extending their writing programmes. Like Gay, Gail believes in children's innate creativity and knows that writing is a rich opportunity to develop their authorship. She advocates the use of children's experiences and ideas as inspiration rather than teacher-prescribed formula. In doing so, children use writing to make sense of themselves and their world.

The examples that follow could contribute to the creation of children's very own "exciting writing" texts, or they could just as readily stand alone as illustrated poetry. While the concept of integrating writing with art is not new, the quality of what is produced varies greatly. Also, the details of how to help children develop high-quality writing and art are often glossed over. The following provides details that open windows to the processes involved.

The big idea

The overarching aim was to help Year 3 children sharpen their writing through poetry and enhance their visual art skills. Poetry, when taught well, helps children carefully select and control the format and use of vivid vocabulary. This discipline of choosing the best possible words in the "right" order to form a pleasing structure (Fisher, 1997) is pertinent at this level. Teachers know that many Year 3 children tend to ramble at length with their new-found powers of written expression. This can lead to lengthy narratives that serve little purpose and lack audience appeal.

The integrated aspect of this unit was deliberately focused on visual art in addition to poetic writing. Gay finds that this connection between visual art and the poetic has considerable merit in terms of producing high-quality work and a sense of pride in children as both artists and writers. What is noteworthy is that one is not sacrificed for the other: both are afforded equal status. As with the poetic writing, the emphasis on visual art is intended to sharpen their focus and help them observe carefully. Through visual art the focus is on the children's artistic skills and their ability to interpret through visual modes what they see. Eisner clarifies that "the arts traffic in subtleties ... learning to see and hear is precisely what the arts teach; they teach children the art, not only of looking, but also of seeing" (2000, p. 9). Seeing, sketching, focusing and later painting or making collage, are all deliberate acts that help deepen children's perceptual skills. Each medium adds to the children's repertoire of expression and leads to new discoveries.

The hook

Gay considered what stimulus might engage the children and act as a catalyst for their creative response. In this case she brought a rooster and two chickens to visit two Year 3 classrooms. As teachers will know, bringing animals into classrooms has instant appeal for children, creating excitement and wonder. Such an atmosphere is ripe for capturing enthusiasm and deepening learning. Instantly the children had many questions to ask and clamoured to touch, hold and watch the birds. Using a range of senses like this is a rich precursor for capturing thoughts and feelings (Costa, 2008), and of course has merit in its own right. Children are naturally drawn to tactile opportunities, and there is nothing like live animals to arouse their innate curiosity. The choice of animals was deliberate, as many city children have little or no experience with animals such as these. Gay's hens are very domesticated, so she had few concerns about them maintaining an obliging sociability in the presence of excited children. Moreover, she realises that vivid experiences such as this are an ideal platform for observational and expressive drawing in order to elicit extended vocabulary and build evocative poetic statements.

Organising for learning

Sketching

The encounter with the birds sparked the focus on sketching, with Gay prompting the children to notice details, textures, contrasts, proportions and the way in which pencils can be used for drawing. For example, she talked to the children about how pencil lines can whisper (soft, light and tiny lines), talk (regular use) and shout (dark, dramatic, thick). Through this she built awareness of tone. She introduced them to techniques of shading, cross-hatching and building textures. The children lay in a circle on the floor around the caged chickens. The moving models of live chickens could be difficult and frustrating for children to capture when it came to details, so various other resources were used to home in on the specific parts of chickens. For example, close-up photographs of beaks, eyes, claws and so forth were blown up and screened on the interactive whiteboard; calendar prints, picture books and stories were also introduced and made available.

While the children sketched they were invited to think of words to describe what they saw. Later this thinking was mined for vivid words and recorded on a flip-chart, which the children could use in their writing. The children's sketches were used to promote dialogue about what works well in drawing and suggestions for where to go next with the class. Thus, the sketching and the development of associated language occurred over several sessions. The revisiting was deliberate in order to deepen the quality of their work; this is returned to in the sections that follow.

Poetry writing

In the next session the focus was on further developing the class word bank based on the close observations already made. To ensure the poetry writing is unique to an individual, certain words and phrases the children suggest are attributed to them alone. This is important to ensure that children's original ideas are celebrated, but are not copied by others, which would have the unfortunate effect of producing rather homogeneous responses. Children have the benefit of seeing and hearing each other's rich language and are spurred to find their own voice.

Gay also takes the opportunity to help children identify cliché and hackneyed expressions. For example, when a child suggested that the chicken looked like a fluffy feather duster, she used this as a teachable moment. With the children she drew attention to how phrases like this are frequently heard and used in speech and writing and therefore lose their power. Children very quickly understood what this means. She challenged them to think more creatively about their very own way of expressing ideas. For example, she would say, "What words come to mind for you when you study the chickens and how can you make your writing your own?"

At Year 3, children often get stuck on rhyming and rather pedantic ways of structuring verse. Gay deliberately introduces the notion of free verse (see also Atwell, 2002). This is done by sharing a number of poems that do not rhyme and discussing the features of these. One of the most powerful examples is the use of a child's poetry (Ranger, 1995). Laura Ranger's poems are all free verse and were written between the ages of 6 and 9. Children are both impressed and encouraged to think that here is a child like them who not only writes beautifully but who has also been published. This resonates for the children as they appreciate that children can become "real" authors and that aspirations can be realised.

She draws attention to the grouping of ideas through stanzas and the notion that poetry is a small piece of writing that says a lot. Children soon comprehend the limitations of having to rhyme and have commented "We are so busy thinking about the rhyming that we forget about using special words; and then they're not as good." She also uses readers' theatre (Hill, 1990) to engage children in reading aloud free verse poems. Again, this models engagement of children using the senses: oracy, gesture, listening, tonality, volume and emphasis. This enactment of the written word instils a love of words: their sound, shape, cadence and the feelings they evoke. In the end, poems do not need to be fully understood or analysed. The most important aspect is how a poem sharpens your thinking and how it makes you feel.

As mentioned earlier, a child's published poetry was shared with the children to help develop their understanding about free verse. In order to enhance the quality of children's writing, Gay drew specific attention to the structure of some of Laura's poems (Ranger, 1995). For example, she shared the following:

MY HOUSE
Rusty Roof
Paint peeling off
Like an old wrinkled person.
Dad's up the ladder
Painting new skin
On the house

The fence is crippled and broken.
Mum's garden is a real mess
Of rosemary and wallflowers
And spiky purple pencils of lavender

In our house
I muck about
In my secret hideout.

I can't tell where it is
Because
It wouldn't be a secret
Any more.

(Ranger, 1995, p. 20; reprinted with permission)

Using the above poem, Gay drew the children's attention to the fact that there are four stanzas and asked them to identify the topic of each stanza, or how the ideas are organised. Children identify that the first is about dad and his chores, the second is about mum and the garden and the last two are about her. Attention is drawn to language features such as similes and metaphor: the old wrinkled person and the new skin; the fence being crippled and the lavender like purple pencils. Such vivid imagery is appreciated as appealing and memorable. They also discussed how they might incorporate such vivid imagery into their own writing.

One of Gay's teaching mantras is that we do not exactly copy other writers but we do learn from them and gain inspiration from the ways in which they weave magic with words. Attention was also drawn to the final stanza and how it reflects the child's personal world. This revealing of the self is like a small gift the writer bestows upon the reader, saying in effect, "Here's a little piece about the inner me I give to you." In addition to its use as a teaching device, the reading of poems by others provides other benefits. McCrary-Sullivan (2005) argues that "the poems we read can take us across boundaries, give us vicarious experience, render the abstract concrete, take us under the skin of the other, generate empathy" (p. 29).

Gay writes a piece of her own and also asks teachers she is working with to write. This models to children that this is a practice to share and that the teacher does not expect children to undertake tasks she is not prepared to engage in herself. In doing so, teachers like Gay build credibility with children and hone their own skills. Teachers need to know what it feels like to write like a poet, and it is only in the crafting of one's own writing that people realise the challenges and joys of such work. This deepens their understanding of what they are trying to teach and how to better support children as they craft their writing.

Children are invited to critique Gay's writing. This is not a polished, published-quality piece, but rather a rough draft that requires editing. At first children responded with praise because children tend to believe that the teacher's model must be of high quality. However, she elicited their help in improving her work. They soon identify repeated words, places where there is too much information and redundant expressions. She repeated the need for poetry to "cut to the bone". This exercise places the children in editing mode and gives them licence to critique writing. It forces them to look beneath the surface and think carefully about the placement, choice and elegance of words.

In a following session the children are provided with a planning scaffold (or writing frame) for their verse. This comprises a title, a hook (which is in the first sentence), a middle (which develops their ideas in two or three sentences) and a conclusion. This naturally reflects three or four stanzas. Children are reminded to incorporate words recorded in the word bank earlier and the sensory impressions gained during the sketching lesson. They are also advised that their title is likely to emerge at the end, as authors cannot predict in advance exactly what will be written because it emerges in the creative act. Certainty and predictability are not the drivers. When engaged in a creative process, whether it be poetry or visual art, we need to be willing to explore the unknown, make errors, refine ideas and tolerate the uncertainty required (Bayles & Orland, 1993).

After being provided with the scaffold, the children are invited to craft their own verses. They are not obliged to use the scaffold; like a conceptual map, it is a support for their writing, especially when it is the first time children have tried free verse. It provides a planning structure, and once some are familiar with a structure they find they can write without it. Others, however, prefer to continue with the structure and hone their skills within it. Some eventually develop their own planning structure that works for their particular verse making.

On the left-hand side of a double-page spread children have their planning scaffold and on the right-hand side they start to craft their writing. This convenient device enables the children to move back and forth, to and from the scaffold, without the distraction of searching for it on a board or another page. At this stage the expectation is that children take responsibility for their writing by themselves in a quiet and uninterrupted manner. The teacher's role is to step back to allow the children space to think, write, ponder and immerse themselves in the writing act. Gay believes it is very important not to rush children. By giving them ample, quality time she conveys the clear message that their work is valuable and deserves their full attention.

At the same time, however, the teacher needs to monitor the room to see if any children are struggling so much that they cannot settle to the task. For example, a child who is known to find writing very difficult can become very distracted and lose self-belief. This is distressing for such a child and is often masked by an array of avoidance behaviour. It is important not to leap to judgement of the child but instead look beneath such behaviour. Gay deliberately works with a child who struggles most in a class (often this is a boy) and scribes for him, eliciting responses through questioning and encouragement of his ideas. Once his piece is completed, she asks if he would like to share his work from the "author's chair". If he is not confident to read it himself, she asks if she can read it for him. The class come to the mat to hear the poem and are invited to respond (the process of responding to each other as writers is an ongoing skill that is developed throughout the year). This process has the effect of boosting a child's confidence, as a struggling child is seldom the first finished. Moreover, the child has the honour of having his or her poem held up as a quality piece of writing. This engenders a feeling of pride and helps grow the child's self-belief.

Once all the children have finished crafting their poems, they are brought to the mat and Gay asks them to carefully choose a phrase, a line or even a few words which they believe represent their finest work. This encourages children's discernment because they have to ascertain the high-quality features of their work. This process informs them as writers and thinkers and can lead to further refinement of their writing. It also has the effect of sharing short pithy pieces, which maximises inclusion and avoids lengthy read-alouds. The message is very clear that every child is to share something of his or her work, but in a supportive and educative community of writers.

Every child is teacher-conferenced by means of a booking schedule. While they wait for conferencing they continue with their art work. As a result there is never a long line of waiting children, nor any reason not to be engaged. However, children do need training in the etiquette of this so that conferences are not interrupted.

Every now and again Gay may stop the class and with the child's permission share a gem from someone's writing. She then asks, "Why have I shared this with you? How might it inform your own work?" In order to conference well with free verse poems, teachers need to be informed about such writing so that they can effectively support children, articulating and unpacking for children what makes such writing work. A simple guideline teachers could use to frame their writing lessons is:

- poems don't have to rhyme
- think where lines begin and end
- say something new
- write the fewest words in the best order (Fisher, 1997, p. 15).

Picking up the visual art again

The children returned to their sketches and these were used as a design source for a larger piece of visual art using paint or collage. Gay made it clear that the images children create do not need to be photographic. Paint and collage lend themselves to simplifying shape and colour to produce abstract images. Details from the drawing were used to create a design shape, but the children were encouraged to literally take artistic licence. Thus, feathers need not be white and tree trunks need not be brown.

Instead, Gay introduced words like "psychedelic" and asked the children what the word means. When they found out and shared the meaning, this spurred them to consider what a psychedelic chicken might look like. This approach to image making is liberating and playful. It helps children to take the leaps of fancy and imagination that make for quirky and unique visual art. Picture books by Peter Wildsmith and Jeannie Baker are a great source of inspiration for this approach.

Painting

With painting, the children create chalk drawings first, which are based on their original sketches but are larger. Coloured chalk is important because it makes children draw boldly and with greater freedom than the fine-edged restraints of pencil. Chalk is also a "no penalty zone" because it is easily rubbed out and painted over. Gay believes that the art works children create are their own visual expressions, with all the joy and freedom implicit in the child's view of the world. Thus, the visual art is obviously the work of a child and should be valued as such. No attempt is made to have children become mini Van Goghs or Monets. Rather, the intention is to build belief in children as developing artists in their own right. This honours the freshness of what children produce and avoids the judgement against adult models of what counts as art. Parents will appreciate that their children's cherished art work (often put on refrigerators at home) celebrates this fresh and honest take on their world.

As with the writing, Gay appreciates that children will never be this age again and their visual art captures the magic of their stage in life. That said, the teacher still has a strong influence on guiding children's learning. Quality art and writing do not emerge from a permissive approach that leaves children entirely to their own devices. In this chapter the teacher is a vital part of the creative process, which could be viewed as a co-constructed series of events. From the decision to bring the chickens to school, through to the sharing of published writing (e.g., Ranger, 1995), the teacher skilfully shaped and refined the children's learning. Wilson (2008) points out that all art activity by children is in collaboration with adults, even if the teacher appears not to intercede. For example, the materials teachers provide in junior classrooms, such as fat brushes, thick crayons and large paper, all shape the outcomes. Teachers should stop fooling themselves that children's artwork is somehow all the children's own work. It is the cumulative outcome of adult–child collaboration, which includes the sequencing of focused initiatives by the teacher (Price, 2010). Rather than asking if teachers play a role in children's art, the following are more fruitful questions:

> We would want to know if the collaborative network is open or partially closed—whether or not students are prohibited from following their interests. We would want to know in what ways power is shared, to know whether kids are permitted to influence the course of art lessons. We would want to know if the contributions of both children and adults are equitable and democratic. We would want to know whose contributions are valued and whose are not, who, adult or child, had imaginative ideas and who did not. We would want to know, who, adult or child, gave and who received assistance. (Wilson, 2008, p. 10)

To introduce the next step, which is the painting of their chalk sketch, Gay believes that the prescriptive forefronting of practical skills is not necessary and in fact inhibits children's painting development. Rather, she invites children to enter painting through an organic, problem-solving approach. As children experience art-related problems, this naturally introduces the teachable moment. The solving of such problems comes from both peers and the teacher, modelling the idea that this work draws upon a class community. This nicely sets children up as experts. In doing so, children are more likely to push the boundaries of what is possible because of the confidence they gain.

A wise teacher knows that children will discover more than can be predicted in advance, given time and opportunity. For example, children are invited to experiment with colour, and in doing so discover blends and hues without the need for a prescriptive lesson on the colour wheel. This freedom to experiment benefits children and is developmentally appropriate. Also, famous artists constantly use trial and error to hone their skills. In addition, no artist's work looks just like another's. This salient point cannot be overemphasised. The painting a child creates should be a reflection of who they are and what they bring to the work. Discovering their unique perceptions, feelings and view of the world is what makes their art important and meaningful. Visual art is a medium through which children make tangible their relationship with their ideas and their media, and each piece is as personal as a fingerprint:

> In making art you need to give yourself room to respond authentically, both to your subject matter and your materials. Art happens *between* you and something—a subject, an idea, a technique—and both you and that something need to be free to move. (Bayles & Orland, 1993, p. 20, emphasis in the original)

In order to raise the quality of paintings, the teacher needs to know the technical problems that might be encountered, and the skills required, and so the topic depicted needs to be carefully thought about. For example, children will persist longer and paint with more detail when the topic is strongly personal, such as climbing trees, swinging on ropes, pets or camp experiences. These contexts are embedded in the child's consciousness, and in visual art the children draw from this deep emotional well in addition to observation.

Fig 10.1 *Painting inspired by climbing trees*

The children are given the primary colours, plus neutrals (white and black) on a newspaper palette. This saves lots of fussing about with plastic palettes, of which there are seldom enough and also require washing afterwards. Newspaper can simply be placed in the paper recycling when finished. Children are given a medium-sized brush to begin with (and no water, to avoid diluting colour). On separate pieces of paper they mix their colours and wipe their brushes clear. Any residues of colour left on the brush have the effect of producing natural blending within the paintings. Gay's knowledge of this effect helps her to shape the children's painting experience. It is important that the painting is not a rushed, "last minute on Friday" session, but instead is a series of focused 1- to 2-hour sessions until the A3 sheets are covered.

Once the paintings are dry, children use a finer brush to add detail. This helps to highlight aspects that would otherwise be lost with larger brushes. It also enables greater control of the paint medium. Again, this models what some adult painters do.

The last stage is to return to the painting with pastel to build up textural qualities. The teacher needs to talk about enhancing contrast through using dark on light and vice versa. This is a chance to play further with colour, to experiment with different media and to enjoy the aesthetic contrasts that emerge from both. In doing so, the teacher is modelling attention to finer qualitative relationships and reflective evaluation. As Eisner states, "attention to such relationships is critical for creating a coherent and satisfying piece of work" (2000, p. 7).

Fig 10.2 *Year 3 poems and paintings*

In order to honour what is completed, the work needs to be displayed with respect. It is also helpful for teachers to add a blurb about the process so that parents, caregivers and other visitors are helped to "read" the work and understand the depth of thinking that underpins the making of art. Too often art is considered a decorative but relatively insignificant learning area. Educating others about the value of what the arts teach is an important part of any school policy and practice. In doing so, community members become aware of the myriad ways in which art fosters persistence, problem solving, informed judgement, critical thinking and depth of perception.

Collage

With collage, the original sketches are photocopied and used as a blueprint for their design. The sketches need to be enlarged so that the collages are manageable and not too fiddly. The children cut around their sketched shape of their chicken (or whatever the focus is) and use this as a pattern to draw around for the base colour. They are given a selection of coloured paper, which they store inside a clear file. The original sketch is also kept in this file for reference. Gay models a collage process using an example she has created, such as a black cat on a white background or vice versa. She then demonstrates how to layer the paper to build texture and to draw attention to features such as eyes and whiskers and fur. Children are shown how to create detail using layered paper shapes rather than pencil lines.

The purpose is not to recreate a photographic replica of the sketch, but rather to artistically interpret and embellish their images. This gives children artistic licence to innovate and experiment with colour and shape. Sometimes it is helpful to restrict the colours provided, as this helps children to contrast hot and cool colours in selective ways and raises the quality of the overall effect. This also underlines the fact that children's art work benefits from having set parameters within which they have freedom to design. It is this very paradox that is the essence of quality in the creative realm (Eisner, 1972).

Another benefit of using collage with children is the tangible, hands-on quality of the work. This way of working is both engrossing and soothing for children, particularly for those children who are physically distractible.

It hones their fine motor skills, and also provides a no-penalty zone for decision making because they can move, change, adapt and refine shapes and colours before committing to a final product. Some children choose to glue as they go, and this has merit for those who struggle to keep materials in hand. In both cases the teacher's job is to draw attention to significant artistic breakthroughs that children make and share these with the class. This builds a cohort of peer expertise and a sense of celebration, raising the overall quality of the final products. It also proclaims to everyone that creativity, risk taking and problem solving are valued.

Conversations about the processes children have used and the purpose of making collage are encouraged. Gay will ask them to look carefully, respond to an image, reinterpret it on collage and think about pleasing shapes and the use of colour. While there are no single right answers, they are challenged to make something special. It is expected that the children will be able to explain what they are learning. This awareness informs them and their parents about the purpose of art. Again, the way in which the results are displayed says much about the value the teacher gives to art work.

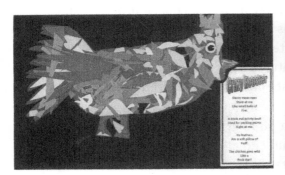
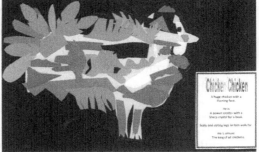

Fig 10.3 *Year 3 poems and collage*

Fig 10.4 *The fire chook*

Fig 10.5 *Poem and collage*

Links to curriculum

A unit like this could well be extended to include spelling (e.g., downloading the application Chicktionary, for instance), science and social studies. In many respects this chapter has less curriculum integration in terms of scope and focus. It is less issues oriented and in some ways, more teacher driven. However, there are many opportunities for negotiation, experimentation and student creativity. Moreover, the teacher scaffolding is an explicit example of the sophisticated pedagogical artistry that ensures quality learning for students. There is no attempt to cover the curriculum as is typical of thematic units. The focus was on two distinct learning areas:

- Visual art: practical skills, developing ideas, communicating and interpreting (levels 1–3)
- English: poetic writing (levels 2–4).

Interestingly, some of the poems indicate that introducing scientific ideas about chickens would be timely in order to rectify confusions about gender!

Conclusion

The visual art and the poetic writing described in this chapter are engaged with in an iterative fashion. This back and forth between the two disciplines enables one to inform the other. It could be argued that the results represent an integrated poetic-graphic message, a multi-modal text that cannot be replicated (Wright, 2010). Honour is given to both the writing and the art work; one does not merely illustrate or describe the other. Gay believes that "The writing is better for the looking and the looking is better for the writing."

In all of the above it is vital that teachers have a go at these approaches themselves. In doing so they will more deeply appreciate the worth of the processes involved and will be better positioned to scaffold children's learning. Teachers will also appreciate the need to move iteratively between the direct teaching of skills and giving children the freedom to explore:

> The approach adopted should be the one most appropriate to the circumstances: teaching style, the subject matter or activity, and the pupils' abilities, attitudes and experience should be considered ... what is important is that pupils gain a comprehensive range of experience, from creative problem-solving to practice in developing skills. (Department of Education, 1978, pp. 58–59)

The teaching of literacy skills is not devalued. In fact the opposite is true, because children are challenged to hone and polish their writing. The strength of Gay's approach is that the skills are taught as needed, and are contextualised in ways that are tangible and meaningful (see also Ewing, 2009). The art work created is rigorously worked and reworked over a sustained period of time. The time given to the collage and painting makes it clear that these areas are valuable in their own right and not mere decorative appendages. It is well known that creating visual art develops qualitative reasoning as well as imaginative cognition (Efland, 2002; Eisner, 2002). Children's capacity to express what they know through the visual form is often deeper than what they can express in words, as visual art provides different boundaries and limitations. For example, it is not limited to a child's vocabulary range or knowledge of literary conventions. Nonetheless, some of the same habits of mind are fostered through visual art as in writing as children seek "rightness of fit" (Eisner, 2000, p. 7) and attend to qualitative relationships (e.g., Does this colour look right here? How can I show texture? Is this the right brush-stroke for the effect I want?). The decisions children make in this context are as important as the choices facing children in writing.

That we privilege writing over visual art across the Western world is testament to the fact that we place greater value on literacy as the pinnacle of what counts as knowledge. It is tempting to lapse into a debate on the relative merits of the disciplines, but this is invariably counter-productive. Literacy is high-stakes in the world and we do our students a disservice if we do not grow their literary power. However, we also do them an immense disservice if we ignore their creative, imaginative, visual skill. Picasso claimed that children are born artists but we educate them out of it (Robinson, 2007). In addition, Wright (2010) argues:

> The schooling process often is at odds with young children's imaginative and creative dispositions. It is biased toward teaching children the rule-bound structured symbol systems, where written letters, words and numbers are seen as a 'higher status' mode of representation over self-derived, visual thinking and reflection. (p. 177)

Gay shows how to address this inequality in status. Both the poetry and the art work are elevated as worthy pursuits that are challenging, engaging and enlightening. The children's views of the world and their imaginative perspectives are brought to life through processes that build skills and foster creativity. This is surely what schools should do.

Art making is risky. It is "like beginning a sentence before you know its ending" (Bayles & Orland, 1993, p. 20). One of the vital elements in creativity is the ability to tolerate the feelings and struggles that come from bringing something new into being. Bayles and Orland argue that "uncertainty is the essential, inevitable and all-pervasive companion to your desire to make art. And tolerance for uncertainty is the pre-requisite to succeeding" (1993, p. 21). These important qualities are fostered when children are engaged in the writing and art making described here. In many respects children are better than adults at this, and the last thing we as teachers should do is stifle their tolerance of the inevitable uncertainties inherent in the creative process.

Acknowledgements

Our thanks go to Cherie Page, Melissa Phillips and Lynette Townsend, whose classes were involved. We are also thankful for Graham Price's feedback on a draft of this chapter.

References

Atwell, N. (2002). *Lessons that change writers*. Portsmouth, NH: Heinemann.

Bayles, D., & Orland, T. (1993). *Art and fear: Observations on the perils (and rewards) of artmaking*. Santa Cruz, CA: Image Continuum.

Costa, A. L. (2008). *The school as a home for the mind: Creating mindful curriculum, instruction, and dialogue* (2nd ed.). Moorabbin, VIC: Hawker Brownlow.

Department of Education. (1978). *Art in schools: The New Zealand experience*. Wellington: Author.

Efland, A. (2002). *Art and cognition: Integrating the visual arts in the curriculum*. New York: Teachers College Press.

Eisner, E. (1972). *Educating artistic vision*. New York: Macmillan.

Eisner, E. (2000, January). Ten lessons the arts teach: Learning and the arts: Crossing boundaries. *Proceedings from an invitational meeting for education, arts and youth funders* (pp. 7–14). Los Angeles.

Eisner, E. (2002). *Arts and the creation of mind*. New Haven, CN: Yale University Press.

Ewing, R. (2009). Creating imaginative, practical possibilities in K-6 English classrooms. In J. Manuel, P. Brock, D. Carter, & W. Sawyer (Eds.), *Imagination, innovation, creativity: Re-visioning English education* (pp. 171–182). Sydney: Phoenix.

Fisher, R. (1997). *Poems for thinking*. Oxford: Nash Pollock.

Hill, S. (1990). *Readers theatre: Performing the text*. South Yarra, VIC: Eleanor CurtainPublishing.

Jones, A., & Middleton, S. (Eds.). (2009). *The kiss and the ghost: Sylvia Ashton-Warner and New Zealand*. Wellington: NZCER Press.

Loane, G. (2010). *I've got something to say: Leading young writers to authorship*. Whitianga: Aries.

McCrary-Sullivan, A. (2005). Lessons from the Anhinga Trail: Poetry and teaching. *New Directions for Adult and Continuing Education, 107*, 23–32.

Price, G. (2010). Competing visions for art education at primary school: A personal view. *Aotearoa New Zealand Association of Art Educators Journal, 20*(1), 28–32.

Ranger, L. (1995). *Laura's poems*. Auckland: Godwit.

Richardson, E. (1972). *In the early world* (2nd ed.). Wellington: New Zealand Council for Educational Research.

Richardson, E. (2003). *Creative processes in language arts teaching*. Auckland: Henderson.

Richardson, E. (2012). *In the early world* (3rd ed.). Wellington: NZCER Press.

Robinson, K. (2007). *Do schools kill creativity?* Retrieved from http://www.youtube.com/watch?v=iG9CE55wbtY

Wilson, B. (2008, August). *The end of child art and the emergence of adult/ kid collaborative conjunctions in three pedagogical sites*. Keynote address to the 32nd International Society for Education through Art world congress, Osaka, Japan.

Wright, S. (2010). *Understanding creativity in early childhood: Meaning making and children's drawings*. London: Sage.

CHAPTER ELEVEN

Conclusion

Deborah Fraser, Viv Aitken and Barbara Whyte

In summary

Readers of this book will recognise that it is a celebration, not only of significant events from the research project Connecting Curriculum; Connecting Learning, but also of innovative New Zealand pedagogy. The Connecting Curriculum; Connecting Learning project initially set out to investigate classroom programmes that used the arts in connection with other curriculum areas. However, case studies of teacher practice showed more than just a variety of connections between the arts and other learning areas. The chapters reveal high levels of democratic pedagogy, whereby teachers and students are actively involved in negotiating and developing the classroom curriculum. Fraser and Paraha (2002) point out that when teachers and students co-construct the learning process, there is a redress of power relationships. This can readily lead to enhanced motivation, relevance and learning for students. These qualities are evident across the chapters in this book.

Fig 11.1 *Working the press during printmaking*

Implications

As the foregoing chapters show, the focus of inquiry generally determines which learning areas are incorporated within an integrated unit. This means that aiming for curriculum coverage in curriculum integration is counterproductive, because the focus of inquiry must be narrowed. In terms of the arts, music and dance did not feature within the case studies presented. Some teachers commented that these subjects were best taught as separate entities to ensure discipline integrity, but this raises the question of when and how such decisions are made. It is no coincidence that drama and visual arts featured, given the interests and backgrounds of the researchers and teachers in the project. Drawing on one's strengths in pedagogy is logical. However, one of the teachers leads her school in music and it was her conscious decision not to incorporate music in her integrated unit. This underlines the importance of not forcing learning areas together, and instead drawing only on those that illuminate the inquiry.

The research project upon which this book is primarily based found that many of the students demonstrated the ability to connect big ideas and learning areas within an integrated unit. This resonates with Nuthall's (2007) classroom research, which also revealed the importance of focusing on the big ideas in teaching. Wilkinson and Anderson (2007) add:

> We need to focus on major questions and problems that provide the most pay-off for students … it is better to invest teaching time and resources in a smaller number of big questions or problems in depth, rather than in covering every aspect of the curriculum at some surface level of understanding. (p. 162)

This pedagogical advice is well supported by the findings of our project. Students are readily drawn to the big ideas in a study, and we enhance their learning when we explicitly focus on these.

A tool called the interactive group activity (see Chapter Five) provided a vehicle for the students to bring their understanding to the surface at a unit's end (Whyte, Fraser, Aitken, & Price, 2012). This tool revealed much more than students' recall and recounting of events. It allowed social negotiation, idea connection and the landing of philosophical insights underpinning the unit. It also required students to use the key competency relating to others as they negotiated their ideas among their group. Such a tool is useful for research and has potential for teachers as part of their assessment repertoire. It also reflects the social constructivist frame of this study.

Some of the integrated units that featured visual art drew community involvement through the use of outside experts and parents who offered skills and support. In one case, the unfortunate incident of a school fire was the catalyst for an arts event that transformed the school environment through art installations. Local artists, parents and other community members contributed time and talent to the arts-inspired resurrection of the school grounds (see Chapter Eight). In another case, the teacher and her class galvanised the local community to raise funds and resources for a school decimated by a tsunami in Samoa (see Chapter Nine). Such community involvement produced motivating home–school partnerships that extended beyond the initial art projects. Both examples provide ample evidence of students' key competencies of participating and contributing at the school and wider community level.

The positioning of students as capable and competent is a salient feature of quality learning within an integrated curriculum. In some cases this happened within a clearly declared fictional adult role (the Mantle of the Expert). Where a dramatic role was used, students pursued their work "as if" they were scientists, writers, designers and so forth, while remaining aware of the "as is" world of the classroom (Aitken, 2008; Edmiston, 2003). The opportunity to operate in the "as if" and "as is" worlds simultaneously encourages students' use of initiative. While the repositioning of the learner as expert was more overt in the classes that used a dramatic role, something similar was observed in all classrooms. In each case, students were scaffolded to take on increasingly adult-like responsibilities and were expected to wrestle with problems.

In drama, teacher-in-role and other dramatic conventions were used to bring a multitude of possible "others" into the classroom to contest thinking, ask for advice or act as an audience. The awareness of some kind of audience, whether fictional or real, lent the learning a sense of intrinsic purpose. It also provided a form of extrinsic motivation to encourage quality. This was also evident in the units that integrated visual art.

Where teachers and researchers repositioned themselves in relation to students, this was found to alter the learning experience. For example, dialogue with students when researchers took low-status roles, such as novices seeking advice, saw students advising adults on the nature of pedagogy and learning rather than merely recalling what they had done (see Chapters Four, Five and Six). Such use of role has benefits for both researchers and teachers when they seek to probe students' learning in ways that invite and position students as expert commentators on their worlds.

Without well-timed tensions or challenges, integrated studies can easily revert to a series of activities that may engage students but not extend their thinking. At various points teachers drew on real-life issues to provoke students' thinking. Some chose issues from immediate social reality (see Chapter Nine). Others, operating through drama, presented real-life issues within a fictional frame. These "grapplings" sustained students' engagement, provided a sense of purpose and raised the quality of thinking. The teacher's ability to discern the opportunities to deepen learning was critical. Introducing tensions and encouraging students to grapple with ideas models knowledge as provisional and open to multiple perspectives (e.g., Chapter Four). Many of the integrated units embraced complex ethical, philosophical and epistemological territory. Opening spaces for students to grapple with big issues, such as the nature of reality and their place in it, required quality questioning and reflection by both teachers and students.

Much attention has been given to the issue of student voice in recent years. Sometimes the rhetoric is more convincing than the practice. We believe that these chapters bring student voice to the forefront. The chapters show students taking on expert roles as they design museums, become archaeologists, explore conflicting perspectives, rebuild a school environment, amass resources for an overseas community in need and become poets and visual artists. These respective roles give them licence to have a say in a curriculum that matters to them. Teachers are not passive in this process, but are actively involved alongside their students, posing questions, speculating and provoking. In treating their students as experts, they raise their expectations of them, which inevitably leads to deepening learning.

Limitations and further research

Four of the case studies focused on using Mantle of the Expert as the approach to integration. While this approach has considerable merit, there are other equally effective ways to enact curriculum integration. A greater range of approaches could have been incorporated. However, the Mantle of the Expert examples presented here provide teachers with useful scaffolds for trying this approach in their own classrooms, and these examples are the first of their kind to be published in this country. In addition, there are three chapters that do not use drama, yet provide equally compelling examples of integration.

It would be interesting to study units that incorporate dance and music in ways that demonstrate the aim of curriculum integration. More can be learned about the benefits and constraints of integrating music and dance. It may be that the disciplines of drama and visual art are somewhat "easier" to integrate. If so, what is it about the issues raised by students and teachers that enable this integration? Are dance and music best taught as separate entities to ensure their integrity? Or, as underlined in this project, does it depend on the nature of the inquiry and the possibilities the inquiry suggests?

A closer focus on how curriculum integration serves the needs of diverse learners could have further strengthened this project. The schools involved were drawn from a range of socioeconomic levels and ethnic compositions, which makes this book highly representative of New Zealand's multicultural society. There are, of course, other groups of students who could be the focus of subsequent projects. For example, it would be useful to research curriculum integration with a particular focus on students with disabilities, and students who are gifted and talented.

It would also be fruitful to further trial the interactive group activity (IGA, mentioned in Chapter Five). It was developed within the research project and proved illuminating with regard to student-to-student negotiation of meaning. The data analysis revealed layers of rich discourse that offer tangible evidence of social constructivist theory in action. Moreover, it showed the connection students made between learning areas, connections that otherwise would not be detected. Too often we make assumptions about what meaning students make, assumptions that may rely on narrow achievement data or anecdotal observations. As Nuthall (2007) reminds us, we need to know how our teaching influences the thinking of our students and find ways to uncover how their beliefs and understanding have changed. Therefore, in addition to its research use, the IGA has potential as a classroom assessment tool. Given the challenges for primary teachers of multiple individual assessments for a whole class of students, the IGA could help teachers collect group data to supplement individual assessment data. Such variety strengthens the validity (and efficiency) of classroom assessment practices. It also emphasises the social context of meaning making.

The arts are frequently underserved and unappreciated in education (Eisner, 2002; Gibson & Ewing, 2011). This makes a book such as this particularly valuable in bolstering the status of the arts. However, the enthusiasm of participants (and researchers) can lead to some overblown claims about the merits of an arts-infused curriculum. Any research project must grapple with this tendency for passionate advocacy to distort one's perceptions. We have endeavoured to mitigate the effects of this by using multiple methods of data collection, and frequent examples of both teacher and student voice. We feel that these chapters provide authentic examples of classroom life.

Critics are likely to point out that these chapters do not report on the hard data of achievement. This, however, was not the intention of the project. There is more than enough such data collection and reporting occurring, as we write, throughout the nation's schools. Moreover, the focus of this book is on learning, not achievement. To conflate the two is to confuse the purpose of education. Not only is learning not the same as achievement, but we do our students a disservice when we believe the two are synonymous. If achievement is the only aim, we perpetuate a version of schooling where education is just another product in the consumer marketplace (Lowe, 2007). If we focus on learning, as evident in these chapters, we see education brought to life through the curiosity, struggles and hard-earned insights of students.

It can readily be argued that from such learning, achievement follows. Studies of Pulitzer and Nobel Prize winners show that, invariably, their goals were intrinsic: they did not primarily strive to be famous or rich, or to win prizes. While it is acknowledged that the motives for achievement are varied and complex, there is widespread agreement that hard work is the universal factor in success. And the sustained passion and drive of the eminent enable them to spend hours and hours pursuing their work (Ludwig, 1995; Simonton, 1994). What stands out among many of the eminent is their deep and abiding passion for pushing the boundaries of knowledge, and their intrinsic pleasure in grappling with challenging ideas. The success that follows in terms of achievement is invariably secondary, and is an outcome, not a goal.

Fig 11.2 *Boy's tree print*

Final remarks

Despite the limitations, this book makes a unique contribution to the fields of curriculum integration and the arts. It provides New Zealand case studies of current practice that reveal the nuances of teachers' pedagogy, including some of the complex challenges they face as they navigate their way through the requirements of the curriculum and the needs of their students. Moreover, it provides classroom data on the types of interactions that deepen learning. This includes verbatim teacher and student comments, as well as researcher observations and analysis. Too few books on teaching and learning have brought together such a range of classroom data that are drawn from the dynamic flux of New Zealand classrooms.

It is important that teachers maintain the courage of their convictions and advocate for deep and engaged learning. Like the teachers in this book, we believe that New Zealand teachers know quality learning when they see it. The case studies provided here show examples of connecting curriculum that are engaging and challenging for teachers and students alike. Integrating curriculum is about maintaining the distinct richness of learning areas, not diluting knowledge into some amorphous and superficial mass. It is also about negotiating with students the method and content of their learning so that they actively participate in a curriculum that matters to them.

References

Aitken, V. (2008). Pedagogical learnings of Borat for make benefit glorious community of drama teachers: What teachers can learn from Borat about frame, position and power when working in role. *New Zealand Journal of Research in Performing Arts and Education: Nga Mahi a Rehia, 1*. Retrieved from http://www.drama.org.nz/?p=394

Edmiston, B. (2003). What's my position?: Role, frame and positioning when using process drama. *Research in Drama Education*, *8*(2), 221–230.

Eisner, E. (2002). *Arts and the creation of mind*. New Haven, CT: Yale University Press.

Fraser, D., & Paraha, H. (2002). Curriculum integration as treaty praxis. *Waikato Journal of Education*, *8*, 57–70.

Gibson, R., & Ewing, R. (2011). *Transforming the curriculum through the arts*. South Yarra, VIC: Palgrave Macmillan.

Lowe, R. (2007). *The death of progressive education: How teachers lost control of the classroom*. London: Routledge.

Ludwig, A. M. (1995). *The price of greatness*. New York, NY: Guilford Press.

Nuthall, G. (2007). *The hidden lives of learners*. Wellington: NZCER Press.

Simonton, D. K. (1994). *Greatness: Who makes history and why*. New York: Guilford Press.

Whyte, B., Fraser, D., Aitken, V., & Price, G. (2012). Interactive group activity: A socially mediated tool for opening an interpretive space in classroom research. *International Journal of Qualitative Studies in Education.* DOI:10.1080/09518398.2012.725140 Retrieved from http://dx.doi.org/10.1080/09518398.2012.725140

Wilkinson, I., & Anderson, R. (2007). Teaching for learning: A summary. In G. Nuthall *The hidden lives of learners* (pp. 153–163). Wellington: NZCER Press.

Index

CPSIA information can be obtained at www.ICGtesting.com
Printed in the USA
LVOW02s2049090614

389253LV00023B/991/P